THE OFFICE AND WORK OF A PRIEST

BY THE SAME AUTHOR

The Office and Work of a Reader

The Office and Work of a Priest

by

ROBERT MARTINEAU
Bishop of Blackburn

MOWBRAYS
LONDON & OXFORD

First published 1972
This revised edition published 1981
by A. R. Mowbray & Co Ltd
Saint Thomas House, Becket Street
Oxford, OX1 1SJ

ISBN 0 264 66528 7

Printed in Great Britain by
Lowe & Brydone Ltd, Thetford, Norfolk

CONTENTS

PREFACE TO THE
FIRST EDITION

THIS book is written as an attempt to make some contribution to the current questioning about the meaning of ministry. Why may not a man who has not been ordained celebrate the Holy Communion? Indeed, why must a man be ordained to exercise the ministry of a priest, if the whole Church is called to be priestly? Men under training at theological colleges are continually asking themselves, and others, what it is for which they are being trained.

It would be easy but, in my opinion, mistaken to give a simple definition of a priest; anyone who satisfied the definition would be a priest, anyone who did not would not be a priest. If it were said, for example, that a priest is a man called by God and ordained by a bishop to celebrate the Holy Communion and to absolve sinners, the definition would be simple enough; but as many questions would be raised as are solved. Ordained priesthood certainly includes this, but is something much greater and more intangible. If, on the other hand, categories of pastoral relationship are used, then questions about the nature of the priesthood of a priest who works in a television centre, a priest-worker or even a cathedral canon are raised. Again, there are people who look at the tasks facing the Church and then say that in the light of the mission of the Church at the present time we need priests to do this or that. This evades all sorts of questions. Who is to say what is the mission of the Church? What happens when a man is ordained? It is easy to say that we need priests to do this or that, but what is a priest?

The dilemma is this. Does the Ordination Service determine what is meant by a priest, in the sense that it says to a man 'This is what you are to be'? Or should we look at the mission of the

Church and ask what sort of ordained ministry is needed and in the light of the answer determine what sort of ordination service there should be? These are profound questions, but I believe that neither is the question we should be asking. Priesthood is a gift of God to the Church and through the Church to the world. By looking at priests and trying to find some pattern in what God enables them to do and in what kind of people, by the grace of God, they become, we can see what it is that God is giving to the Church through its ordained priesthood. To do this thoroughly would require a far longer volume than has been written and there are many aspects of priesthood which are not mentioned. Nothing, for instance, has been said about the Religious Life and no attempt has been made to describe the work of a Diocesan Director of Education, a Stewardship Adviser or a Youth Chaplain. No attempt has been made to be exhaustive; but there are qualities which priests in different contexts have in common and it is to these qualities that we should look if we seek the meaning of priesthood.

It was from B. K. Cunningham, Henry McGowan and Frank Sangster that I derived my early impressions of what priesthood could mean. If anything of the inspiration which they passed on is conveyed in these pages, I shall be thankful. I am indebted to many friends for comments and criticism, for factual information and for new insights. I am grateful to Canon Lloyd Rees, the Reverend Tony Williamson, Canon Edwyn Young, the Reverend Neville Smith, Canon Basil Moss, Dr Michael Higgins, the Reverend David Muston, the Chaplain of the Fleet and the Chaplain-General of the Forces, and many others for information and also for ideas directly or indirectly given. None of these can be held responsible for any opinions expressed. Students at Westcott House, Cambridge, over the last six years have helped me to ask questions about the office and work of a priest; some of the material in this book has been the substance of talks given there.

November 1971   R.A.S.M.

PREFACE TO THE
REVISED EDITION

In this revised edition of what was written nine years ago, the opportunity has been taken to refer to a number of changes in the pattern of worship provided for by the Alternative Service Book. In particular, the wording of the Ordination Service is different from that in the Book of Common Prayer. There have also been developments in the training of Ordination candidates to which reference is made.

December 1980. R.A.S.M.

I

THE SERVICE OF GOD IN AN IMPERFECT WORLD

THE meaning of priesthood can only be considered in the light of the purpose of God for the Church. Priesthood belongs to the Church and priests are called by God to serve his purposes through the Church, and to enable the Church to serve his purposes in the world. The Church has been called into being by God to serve the ultimate end of his will for man. That ultimate end is what the scripture calls the Kingdom of God. 'The Lord is King' is the primary message of scripture and of the Church. But if God is King, in fact and not only by right, then we should expect all things to be good; nature and man would obey his will. It is self-evident that this is not the case. There may be any of three reasons why man does not do the will of God. He may not know what that will is; he may know but not want to do it; he may know and want to do God's will, but finds he has not the power in himself. One activity of God in establishing his reign on earth must be the declaring of his will, and one way in which men have believed that he does this is through particular people. In the record of the Old Testament, the prophets were such people. The mark of a prophet was that he could say 'Thus says the Lord'. His message might take the form of announcing the will of God in the form of a command, or of pointing out how a command already given was being ignored or deliberately broken. It might explain what the already expressed will of God involved in a new situation. Equally it might explain what God would do in response to man's action, either in justice or mercy. In these senses, the prophet was seen as a man who understood the mind of God or who was so filled by the spirit of God that he could speak through him. But while the mark of a prophet was that he declared the will of God, part of his task was to encourage people to do it. This might be by warning of the consequences of disobedience, or by the promise of blessing to those who obeyed. The reign of God would really be established when instead of a written code of law which man must obey, God would plant his law in the hearts of men who would then want to do his will.

The work of the prophet, then, was the work of revealing the word of God. Where men understood that word and wanted to do God's will but found themselves prevented from doing it by their weakness, their past or their circumstances, it called for more than a prophet to help. When men looked back on their own past and saw where they had not kept the will of God, it was beyond their power to make good what was lacking. To reconcile what was with what ought to be called for more than revelation of God's will and nature. The priest sought, by prayer and by sacrifice, to do this. Prayer was one means by which God was asked to bring about what ought to be. Sacrifice, certainly in later Old Testament times, was an attempt to atone for imperfection. However imperfect might have been the gratitude or the penitence or the desire of the person for whom the sacrifice was made, the offering itself had to be without blemish. Prayer and sacrifice acted as bridges between the will of man and the will of God, indeed as bridges between man and God.

Prophet and priest, therefore, were two necessary forms of ministry in an imperfect world. They could only minister among those who acknowledged their right to do so, that is to say among those who recognized the sovereignty of God. The Jews believed themselves to have been chosen both to declare that the Lord is King, and also in their national life to be a people ruled by God. In the life of Israel as a whole, God's Kingship would be embodied. Two glaring facts remained true. Other nations did not accept the Kingship of the God of the Hebrews, and they themselves fell far short of realising it. Someday, God would send his anointed one to make the hope of his complete reign a reality.

The teaching of Jesus is centred on the Kingdom of God. He declared that the Kingdom of God was at hand. His acts of healing, his readiness to declare a man forgiven of his sins, the bringing of sight to the blind, and life to the dead, all these were signs of the activity of God among men. God was not distant and inactive. The words of Jesus revealed the will and the nature of God and the ways of his working; his actions revealed the presence of God among men. In his very life and words, prophet and priest come together. 'Ye have heard that it hath been said . . . but I say unto you . . .' (Matt. 5.22, 23, etc.); and again 'if I with the finger of God cast out devils, no doubt the Kingdom of God is come upon you' (Luke 11.20). The coming of the Kingdom does not wait for man's turning to God. In Christ, it has come to men. The acts of healing and the words of grace were evidence that it had come. The barriers which stood in the way of a full life in fellowship with the eternal God of love were broken down— barriers of frailty, ignorance, sin and death.

As Son of Man, Jesus acted in obedience to the will of God. The barrier of human imperfection was broken down in him, for his whole life was one of self-giving. In an imperfect world, self-giving involves suffering and deprivation. Perfect self-giving involves unlimited suffering and complete deprivation, and complete deprivation for man means death. The solidarity of man is such that the sin of one causes suffering to another. The nature of love is that it gives of itself for the sake of another. Love takes upon itself the weakness and the faults of others. In Jesus Christ we see these things brought together as nowhere else. The occasion when the sin of man is seen in supreme clarity is also the occasion when the love of God is seen most clearly in action. The difference between what is and what ought to be is not explained away. On the contrary these two opposites, sin and love, are brought together; they are reconciled in Christ. That love absorbed and overcame sin is assured not only by the fact that Christ freely and lovingly accepted man's rejection to the point of death, but also by his resurrection. The Ascension is the assurance that the unconquered love of the risen Christ is also the sovereign power of God. To the assertion 'The Lord is King' the Christian adds the assertion 'Christ is Lord'.

Jesus called the Church into being to continue his work. Call and commission are essential elements in the nature of the Church. 'You have not chosen me, but I have chosen you' (John 16.16) and again 'As my Father hath sent me, even so send I you' (John 20.21) are typical of the call and commission of Christ to the Church. The Church is not a collection of people who think that the best way of serving the world would be to apply the principles of Christ's teaching, however true that may be. It is a collection of people who have responded to his call to come to him and, having come, are ready to accept his commission to go into the world to proclaim the good news. Between the coming and the going there is an event which can be described in many ways; some may call it conversion, others an encounter with Christ. The early disciples met and saw and heard Jesus of Nazareth; after the first Easter they proclaimed that the same Jesus whom they had known, who had died on the cross was alive, risen and ascended. They acknowledged his sovereignty and accepted it for themselves. In doing this, the body of them became a body in which Christ was allowed to reign. In other words the Church came into being both to proclaim and also to embody, or to reveal in visible form, the Kingdom of God; its task is to work for its acceptance and embodiment in the world. Christians believe that the remedy for the world's ills is the willing acceptance of the rule of God, made known in Jesus Christ. This is an approach different from that of the social reformer who first sets out the benefits which it is desired to achieve and then devises a programme to achieve them. Thus some slogan such as 'liberty, equality and fraternity' becomes the guiding principle, or some principle such as 'from each according to his ability and to each according to his need' becomes the motive; a party or body of people is then organised to pursue the end. The Church is called to proclaim and embody the sovereignty of a Person not of a principle. The benefits such as peace and prosperity and the brotherhood of man will come as consequences of obedience to God revealed in Christ.

The whole Church, not just part of it, is called to do this work in the world. The whole Church is called to be a body in which Christ reigns and so to reveal to the rest of the world what society could become if Christ were acknowledged as King. The work of the prophet in pointing out the difference between what is and what ought to be, including what men are and what men ought to be, was done in its fulness in and by Jesus Christ. The prophetic work of the Church is related to him; it is the work of the whole Church and is done both by what Christians say and by the life of the body which they comprise. The work of atoning for the imperfection of this world was also done in its fulness. The self-offering of his life was complete. All that the priests had tried to do, he had done. The bridge between man and his will and God and his will was established in Jesus Christ.

The work of God in the world is the same as it always was, only with a new point of reference. It is still the work of pointing the difference between what is and what ought to be, only this means pointing to Christ. It is still the work of bringing what is and what ought to be together, and this again means relating everything to Christ who has done this perfectly. The three reasons given at the beginning of this chapter why men do not do the will of God, or acknowledge the sovereignty of Christ, remain the same. They may not know, which calls for the evangelist and the teacher. They may know about Christ and his will but reject it, which calls for a clearer showing of Christ's love in word and in deed. They may know about and want to serve Christ, but find they have not the power in themselves. This calls for the ministry of the grace of God. All this is God's work which he empowers the Church to do. The ordained ministry is called and set aside and enabled by God to do this to the Church and to lead the Church in doing this to the world.

There are clearly many kinds of ministry, and they overlap;

by no means all the ministry of the Church is ordained. Readers, for example, share very fully in the ministry of declaring the Word, that is to say the ministry of pointing men to Christ. The priestly ministry relates particularly to that of reconciling men to God and the peculiarly priestly attribute is that of trying to see all people (and all things) in their relationship to God and to help them into that relationship. The priest is concerned to see people at birth, growing up, marriage and death, in sickness and sin, in times of perplexity, vocation, triumph and despair, all in relation to God in Christ. He is concerned to see the body of the Church in right relationship to God, which involves its worship; in mutual charity and harmony, which involves the structure of the Church in every form; and in right relation to the rest of the world, which means its strategy of service and outreach. In this last respect, he is concerned to see the world brought into right relation to God which is the meaning of mission.

All this is related to Christ's completed work of reconciliation, of making possible the bringing of all things and people into right relation to God. The Holy Communion is both a demonstration of how Christ reconciled the world to God, and also a means by which the link between what he has done and what we want to do is established and strengthened. In this way, the celebrating of the Holy Communion is an essential part of the priestly work of the Church.

The ministry of a priest is a ministry of the grace of God. This does not mean, though it has at times been so believed, that God limits his activities in any way or channels his grace only through the ministry of a priest. It does mean that God uses the ministry of a priest to be a channel of his grace; so that what is effected is done by the power of God and not of man alone. It is here that the fundamental meaning of priesthood must be understood. God is a God who acts as well as speaks. He calls men and women to act for him. He also acts through them. At a time when there is an impatient and right demand that the Church should be doing more in the world and for the world, it is even more important that the Church should strengthen its hold on the doctrine of grace. It is only by the action of God that what is can be transformed into what ought to be.

2

TRADE, PROFESSION OR CALLING

THE implied distinctions in the title of this chapter take us at once to the heart of the question 'What is a priest?' Is he to be classified by what he does, or by what he stands for, or in respect of the reason for his being what he is? The very words 'trade or profession' imply a distinction of status, and carry us near to a false judgement of values. The Christian does well to remember that if he uses this classification, then his Master would be classified as a tradesman. If we avoid the idea of trade or profession and speak of priesthood as a calling, then we must be most careful to avoid any suggestion that other ways of life are not also callings. Many other ways of life, not just a few special ones, can be seen as a calling. In the words of the Methodist Covenant Service, 'Christ has many services to be done; some are easy, others are difficult; some bring honour, others bring reproach; some are suitable to our natural inclinations and temporal interests, others are contrary to both. In some we may please Christ and please ourselves, in others we cannot please Christ except by denying ourselves. Yet the power to do all these things is assuredly given us in Christ, who strengtheneth us.' (*The Book of Offices*, Methodist Publishing House, ad loc.)

The significant fact about this variety of service to which Christ may call us, is that it applies to all who would be faithful Christians. Every Christian has a vocation. A man cannot expect to follow Christ and not be given something to do for him and to become for him. Within the great variety of service to which God calls, the life and work of a priest has a particular place; it represents to the Church itself and to the world outside one special aspect

9

of the life and work of the Church as a whole. But the use of the word calling, or vocation, does not exclude the description trade or profession; every honourable trade or profession can be the way in which a man fulfils his vocation. There lurks at the back of the mind of some people the thought that because a person follows a certain way of life as a vocation, that he does it for love and not for money. These half-truths are misleading. Few, if any, are priests for the sake of the money; equally, any attitude of being wholly above such a sordid thing as money can lead to a false sense of pride. The labourer is worthy of his hire, as the scripture reminds us, and in a Church where for the most part priests are married men, they have a right to expect a reasonable stipend for full-time service.

To speak of any occupation or way of life as being a calling implies someone who calls and, in the case of a calling to priest-hood, this means a belief in a God who calls. This is a very far-reaching assertion of belief. If God can call a man to a particular way of life, then he is a God who has a particular will and not just a general will for mankind as a whole. It is one thing to believe that God created time and space, but quite another to believe that at any point in time and space he should want one person to do this rather than that, when either choice would be judged honourable and good. More than this, such a God must convey his particular will to the person for whom he has it, and the person whom he calls must be able to know that this is the call of God. It is easy to talk about vocation, but it implies asser-tions about God and his relations with men which can be accepted or dismissed far too glibly.

It is because we believe in a God who is personal that we can believe that he has even a general will for mankind. The will of God is not the same as a set of maker's instructions; in such a case if we follow them the world would work, and if we ignore them things would go wrong. It is quite true that, in fact, this does apply to the will of God when it has been expressed in the form of laws or instructions. It is true that self-interest enters in, and obedience is sometimes commended on the ground 'that it may be well with thee' or 'that thy days may be long in the land which the Lord thy God giveth thee' (Deut. 6.3; Exod. 20.12). The will of God is the way God wants things to happen and people to behave. The ultimate end of doing the will of God is to please him. Self-interest commends honesty because it is the best policy for us. The man who believes that human honesty is part of the will of God tries to be honest in order to please God. The Christian believes that the will of God has been made known in the life and teaching of Jesus, and through the guidance of the Holy Spirit in the Church. Thus all Christians are called to be saints, to be witnesses to the love of Christ, to be pure in heart, to forgive others and so on. This will of God is general both because it applies to all people and also because all of it applies to each person. We do not have to choose between being pure in heart and forgiving others.

The particular will of God applies when a man is convinced that God wants him to do this rather than that; to remain single, for example, rather than to marry; to teach rather than undertake some other work, or whatever the choice may happen to be. The choice here is exclusive. By following one path, some other paths are excluded. For this reason, a man wants to be very sure that he is right in believing that some particular way is the call of God to him. How does such a call come to a man and how can he be sure it is God's call?

Some people seem to have their future determined for them by birth. As society is organised at present, children born into certain families have little control over their future unless at some point they contract out of the consequences of their family status. The principle applies far more widely than just a few hereditary occupations. Without passing any moral or value judgement, it is natural that sons of certain families will follow in their father's footsteps as they inherit the family estates, business and responsibilities. The limitations on freedom of choice are considerable both in such a situation and also among families who live in places which are so dependent upon one trade or industry that economic and social pressures largely determine a child's future. It is not necessary to believe that it is the particular will of God that a child should become a farmworker, coal-miner or fisherman just because he was born in a certain place within a certain family. Increasing mobility of population and improved educational opportunities are changing the pattern and enlarging the scope of a man's choice of occupation. But it is possible either to accept the situation and serve God faithfully in it, or to rebel. The rebellion may take the form of a lifetime of kicking against the pricks, or of a deliberate effort to change the course of one's life. The acceptance also may be a matter of resignation to the situation or of willing service to others as a freely accepted responsibility of status. In this last case, the situation is accepted freely as being that in which God wants to be served; but equally he who tries to step out of the situation may do so because he believes God wants to be served by him in some other way.

Then again, there are those who have responsibilities given them by election or selection to an office by others. The fact that they sought that position is only a part of the picture; others may also have wanted and applied for it. Eventually one person is selected and he becomes a foreman, a Member of Parliament, a judge or a company director. His responsibilities may extend far beyond the persons who selected him; indeed, he is likely to have responsibilities towards those who wished to choose somebody else. Here again it is not necessary to believe that God has overruled the process of election to ensure that one man rather than another should be chosen, but it is possible freely to accept the fact that one can and should serve God in the particular situation. A Christian judge or a Christian trades union leader can rightly feel that he is answerable to God for his decisions and that, whatever may have been the method of his selection, it is now God's will that he should serve him in this position.

It is perfectly possible for a man to receive a sense of call, which he understands to be a call from God, in a time of prayer at some definite moment. The story of the call of Samuel is commonly quoted as a biblical parallel to such an experience. It is worth noting that even in the biblical story it was through the words of the man Eli that Samuel was able to understand the call. If a man prays sincerely, an awareness that God's will for him means choosing one path rather than another is to be expected. It by no means follows that this is the only, or even the normal, way in which God calls an individual to some special form of service.

One of the more common ways in which men become aware of a call to priesthood is through the life and example of some other priest. When self-giving and joy, holiness and human understanding, are seen to be combined in one person, others are likely to be attracted. The priest through whom God works to call another may well be unaware of the fact. His life acts both as a challenge and as an inspiration; call and encouragement are combined. The process through which the man who is so called must go may be a very long one. He must learn for himself the source of the joy, the secrets of holiness, the discipline of self-giving which he has seen in another. He must ask himself and others whether these cannot be had in some other walk of life and whether it is in the life and work of a priest that God wants him to give himself in service. He must recognise that being human it is likely that his motives may be mixed, and that there are some attractions in the life of a priest which are very human and worldly. He must ask himself whether it is because he would like to be respected in the way he respects this priest, and for whose sake. Yet when all is said, if Christ is alive in the heart of one priest and speaks and acts through him, then those who respect the man are respecting Christ and those who want to be his imitators are wanting to be imitators of Christ.

Some men feel themselves called to priesthood because it appears to offer opportunities for serving others in a fuller way. This is a very commonly expressed motive. It is the more interesting because the days are gone when the parish priest was the source of most forms of service or social aid in his parish. New forms of social service and of personal counselling are emerging. Responsibility for social security is part of national policy. Industries and communities also are ready to employ welfare officers. Yet with all this expansion of service to others there is a searching for something deeper and fuller which men believe can be offered in priesthood. They are prepared to forego some of the freedom and material rewards of one way of service because of the richer satisfaction that the priestly calling appears to offer. It is not that priestly service is seen as an alternative to marriage counselling or social welfare; on the contrary these are recognised as very necessary counterparts. The work of a priest is seen as going beyond anything that man can offer and thus as a contemporary expression of the life of him who gave himself for others.

It is seldom that one motive only draws a man to offer himself for the life of a priest. The call to every Christian is to live a life of self-giving love and in an imperfect world such self-giving love will involve a measure of sacrifice and suffering, of hardship and of willing deprivation. The desire to accept all this freely for the sake of Christ who accepted it freely for us can be a very strong desire. The man who feels this must ask himself carefully whether he desires this for Christ's sake, or whether he enjoys hurting himself or even whether he wants others to see how much he has given up in order to live as a priest. The devil is very ready to take an earthly desire or some natural expression of our emotional development and persuade us that this is a call from God. The call to priesthood and the call to life in a religious community need to be prayerfully examined, with the help of others, so that the will of God may be made clear.

Another way in which the call of God may come to a man is through the spoken suggestion of another person. It may be a direct word from a chaplain to a student, or from a priest to a parishioner. It may be more indirect as when, for example, the possibility of ordination is suggested during preparation for confirmation. With the growth of the non-stipendiary, or

Auxiliary Pastoral Ministry, the calling may come from within the parish where a man might serve. Not only the Vicar but the Parochial Church Council also will be involved, and the reactions of a man's employer will help to clarify whether the suggestion is indeed a calling to serve God in this special way. It may well be that a man's witness to Christ would be greater, in his place of employment, as a layman than as a priest.

Over against the many ways in which a man may feel that God is calling him to be a priest there are many fears which hinder him from responding. While some men may so respect a priest they know that they want to serve God in the same way, others are put off by what they have seen in a priest, not only from any desire for priesthood themselves but even from the outward practice of the Christian religion. There are others who wonder if they are called to priesthood but fear that they will have to spend their lives raising money from reluctant givers to achieve ends which are secondary to the Gospel: the repair of a church roof, the improvement of an organ, new robes for the choir. They fear that they will spend their time largely with small groups of inward-looking and elderly people. They fear that they may get stuck in a backwater because of what they deem to be the cumbrous structure of the Church and that they will be overlooked. It is easy to say that priests should be humble enough to be overlooked and it would be true to say that they are not, in fact, overlooked; but the fear in some remains and they look to a more modern and secular structure in which to find the outlet for their desire to serve God and their neighbours. Other men, with family commitments, may be willing to make sacrifices themselves but for the highest motives are unwilling to subject a wife and family to some of the inevitable consequences of a clerical household. Compared with many occupations which a priest might otherwise have undertaken after suitable training, clerical stipends are modest. Some clerical houses are over large. Since in the parochial ministry a parish priest should live among his people in the parish, it means that often a man is taking his wife and family to an area where otherwise he would not choose to live. This is no judgement either on the man or on society; it is just facing facts. If a man is already married, he and his wife must look squarely at the fact that a clerical family has much less privacy than most other families and that in the evenings, when other fathers are normally free to give time to their children, clergymen are likely to be most fully occupied. If there are already children in the home, and the family is accustomed to worshipping as a family, the fact that family worship will no longer be possible in the same way must be honestly faced. For a married man, in short, any vocation to the priesthood must be seen as a joint vocation to a new way of life which, if accepted as the will of God, must be joyfully accepted by both.

There are men who are so conscious of the presence of God in the ordered worship of the Church that they want to spend as much of their life as possible in such activity, and so feel that priesthood would be better than any other way of life. There are others who see only the outward side of a clergyman's life, and can of necessity know nothing of its more hidden joys and frustrations. Some are so keen to tell others the secret of the joy they find in the gospel of salvation that they see ordination as opening the door to a lifetime of preaching the good news. It may well be that God is calling some of these to be laymen and to exercise their ministry as Readers. A priest's life is by no means all spent worshipping in church, or overtly preaching the gospel. What is certain is that it is just not possible to know in advance what life as a priest will involve for any particular person. The element of faith or trust must be there from the start, a readiness to be led all the way without having the future neatly mapped out. What is remarkable is how many men are wholly convinced that God is calling them to this life, when they themselves know so little of what it will involve. They know their school or college chaplain, they believe the Christian faith and have experience which they interpret as an awareness of the presence of Christ, but their connection with any parish life may be tenuous. Of the reality of their vocation, however, there can be little doubt.

What criteria are there, if any, by which a man can distinguish between his own inclination (or disinclination, for that matter) and a call from God? There is none that can be absolutely sure. A living faith is not founded upon a dead certainty, but there are some signposts. On the negative side, the fact that a man has had no strange supernatural experience which he could identify as a divine call is no criterion at all. On the positive side, a call to priesthood will result in a growing awareness of Christ's love for all men and a readiness to share that love. Christ's love is without limit, either in its extent or its depth. A call to the priesthood will, if real, result in a growing sympathy for others, a growing anxiety that they should know and love Christ and a diminishing criticism of their faults. A call to priesthood will be seen more and more clearly as a life-long commitment, for it is a call to respond to love in a particular way. In any case the Christian life itself is a life-long commitment. It is Christ's love which constrains us (2 Cor. 5.4) and that is incompatible with trying it out for a few years to see how it works. It is also a response to love which attaches no other conditions. In some cases, it would seem most likely that a man's ordained ministry will be spent in a certain geographical or cultural area because he has been given gifts which others lack and which can be used in such areas. But a readiness to go anywhere, home or abroad, town or country, is one criterion by which a man may judge his sense of vocation.

Since a priest's life will largely be spent in the structures of the visible Church, a call to priesthood will result in a growing conviction that the Church is being used by God to set forward his Kingdom on earth. There are many weaknesses in the structure of the Church, and many weak people among its members. But God has called the Church into being for his purposes, and in its life his children are called to find him and love him and serve him. The Church as a whole is called to proclaim the Kingship of Christ, to reveal his love, to build up his Body. The fellowship of the Church is no mere like-mindedness but the fellowship of the Holy Spirit; it is something out of this world. The man who is called to be a priest will love, desiring the best for, the Church more and more.

But the element of faith remains. A man cannot expect before ordination, or at the beginning of his ministry, the vision or mature understanding that comes from experience. To follow the guidance of God is essentially an act of faith, a readiness to go forward without knowing what lies ahead.

As the disciples on the Emmaus road had to wait till the end of their journey before they realised who had been their companion, so a priest may, at the end of a lifetime of faithful service, realise in retrospect the certainty of a vocation which at the time was accepted in faith. This will be realised not just by a sense of joy and personal satisfaction in life, though there is plenty of that; nor by looking back on having made a success of a parish, for success in that sense is almost indefinable and, in any case, any so-called success is the work of God. It will be realised rather by a knowledge that one has been used by God to enable the Church to proclaim the sovereignty of Christ in word and action, and to enable individuals to acknowledge that sovereignty in their own lives and so come to be in right relationship with God.

3

SELECTION AND TRAINING

A PRIEST is a man who is called, chosen and sent. We have, in the previous chapter, thought about the call from God and how it may be recognised. This call needs also to be recognised by the Church in which the priest serves. When a man is convinced, or even begins to consider, that God is calling him to the life and work of a priest, he should talk the matter over with his parish priest or the chaplain who serves the body of people to which he belongs. Together they can examine what is likely to be involved in the possible course of training and the qualifications needed before the training could be undertaken. The man himself must consider how his domestic relationships will be affected, especially if he has a wife and family; for the life and work of a priest cannot be separated, and his home is part of his life. If, after consultation with his parish priest, he is still convinced that God is calling him to be a priest, he should approach the bishop of the diocese where he lives or the priest (usually called the Diocesan Director of Ordinands) whom the bishop has appointed to act for this purpose. The sense of call is all the time being tested, but the particulars are now thoroughly examined. If it seems right to the parish priest and the Director of Ordinands, then the man will be referred to the bishop who has the responsibility of 'sponsoring' the candidate for a Selection Conference. The bishop is not promising to ordain the man, nor is he saying to the selectors 'I think this man should be trained for ordination, but what do you think?' He is saying that in his opinion there is enough evidence of a call for it to be tested further, and that if the Selection Conference recommends training for ordination and if he concurs with that recommendation, he will exercise pastoral oversight of the candidate up to the time of his ordination either in that diocese or by some other bishop elsewhere. The candidate has a bishop to whom he can turn and on whose prayers he can rely.

The Director of Ordinands or the bishop himself then asks the Advisory Council for the Church's Ministry, commonly known as ACCM, to invite the candidate to a Selection Conference. The candidate is asked to explain a number of points in an application form and to submit the names of people who will act as referees. In due course he arrives at the Selection Conference (on a Monday afternoon) and finds himself living with some fifteen or so other candidates, four selectors (chosen from a list of men nominated by the bishops) and one of the selection secretaries of ACCM. They live together, eat together, pray together and talk together until the Thursday morning. This is a conference to try to discover to what form of service God is calling each man. It is not an examination to see if a man is good enough; none of us is good enough. Except for the ACCM secretary, everyone is likely to be a stranger to everyone else. What is remarkable is how in under three days each person allows himself to be known by all, and knows himself better also, and friendships are formed which are lasting. The selectors comprise one senior priest (usually an archdeacon or a suffragan bishop) who acts as chairman and who talks with each candidate about how God has been making his call known and how the candidate has responded (in prayer and in other ways) to this sense of call. There is an experienced parish priest who seeks to know how aware the candidate is of the implications of a pastoral ministry in a parish, and to consider whether it is to such a pastoral ministry that God is calling him. There is a selector who is concerned whether the candidate can think and express himself sufficiently clearly not only to undertake the necessary training but to explain the faith to others in ways they will understand. There is a layman (man or woman) who tries to discover how much the candidate knows about the world which God is calling the Church to serve, and whether he can envisage the candidate in five or ten years time serving God and his Church best as a priest or as a layman. The ACCM secretary, who makes his own assessment out of his experience of very many ordinands and who keeps in touch with the candidate throughout any period of training that may follow, is the only selector who has seen the references that have been given. Each selector sees each candidate individually, but there is no general interview; this is not an examination board. There are talks, discussions and exercises on different aspects of the life and witness of the Church today. The candidates will have told their vicars and so prayer will be made in a dozen or so parishes that the will of God may be made clear; the selectors will also have asked others to pray for the conference. In this way the whole conference becomes an activity of the Church seeking the guidance of the Holy Spirit.

When the candidates leave, the selectors remain to make their recommendations. In doing this, they have the help of the references which are now read; thus indirectly the referees assist in the process of selection. There are various forms in which the selectors give their advice to the bishops. A man may be recommended for training, with or without some condition being attached; such a condition might be the completion of a course of study which is being currently pursued, or that adequate financial arrangements can be made for the man's wife and family, or some other condition. A man may be 'not yet recommended' if the selectors feel that there should be an opportunity for the further development of a candidate's ability or character before they can in confidence recommend him for training. They may feel that God is not calling him at this particular moment to leave what he is doing in order to train for the priesthood or that the call is not yet clear. Such a candidate might well be encouraged, if his sense of calling to the priesthood persists, to come to another conference in a couple of years' time. The selectors may feel of some men that it is as laymen that they can best serve the Church and will advise the bishop that such men should not be trained for ordination. When all the recommendations have been made and the selectors have returned home, the ACCM secretary communicates to the bishop of each candidate the conclusions which were reached by the selectors about that candidate. The bishop tells the candidate what decision he has made as a result of the advice given. Probably through the Diocesan Director of Ordinands, advice will be given as to the nature of the training and the place where it shall be taken.

The exact details of training and qualifications required change as opportunities offer and needs arise. In broad terms it can be said that a younger candidate is expected to undergo a five- or six-year course, which would include a university degree and two or three years at a theological college depending on whether the degree was in theology or some other discipline. There are some four-year courses where the degree in theology is taken from a theological college and there is a concurrence of ordination training and degree course. There are also courses for those with less formal academic qualification, whose abilities lie in other directions. For older candidates there is a two-year course at a theological college with a modified ordination examination. All these courses are residential and full-time. In addition, there are several centres at which non-residential courses are based; these provide not only for the non-stipendiary ministry but also for those offering for full-time service. They make training possible for men who have family commitments for whom an extended period of residential training would be difficult. There is also a system, known as the Aston Training Scheme, which uses tutors all over the country to undertake a large measure of preliminary or initial training. Indeed, the whole system is both under constant review and also becoming more flexible. The Church assists all candidates who cannot meet the cost of their training from their own resources and from grants; but ACCM does not have authority to make grants for the maintenance of a candidate's wife and family. Such candidates may, however, receive help from the annual 'Train a Priest' appeal made through the *Church Times*.

The purpose of the training at a theological college is to equip the candidate to think and to pray theologically. As he does this, he is at the same time putting his sense of vocation to the test. Thus the basis of the training is a knowledge and understanding of the bible, the context in which each part was written and the message that part conveyed. When any part of that message is seen to be relevant today, something theological is being said about the nature of man and of society and of God's dealing with each. Since the priest is a preacher of the Word, training for priesthood involves a thorough grounding in the bible; this may be given as part of a university course, or in the theological college itself. It will include some acquaintance with the Greek text of the New Testament and a detailed examination of one or more books of the bible. This detailed study and all the academic work in studying theology brings the student to face a problem which will be with him all through his life as a priest. On the one hand academic openness requires that everything, without exception, shall be exposed to question and criticism; this must include the words of scripture and also the processes of thought by which men arrive at conclusions. On the other hand, the student would not be where he is unless he had responded to a call which he believed to be from God. This tension between commitment and critical inquiry is part of the essence of life lived by faith and, if understood and accepted, helps the student to steer a course between fussy indecision on the one side and bigotry on the other. Naturally it is hoped that after ordination the priest will continue to give to the scriptures as a whole the same detailed and critical study that, as a student, he was required to give to one part.

The course at a theological college includes the study of Christian doctrine which involves, among other things, a study of the forms in which the faith has been expressed in the Church and the development of these forms. There is a study of heresy, the distortion of doctrine to fit an incomplete picture or an inadequate understanding of the facts. The development of the doctrine of the person of Christ is the record of the Church trying to think theologically about the significance of Jesus. If the priest is to proclaim the Christian faith, he needs to be able to think and express himself clearly, presenting neither an incomplete nor distorted picture of the facts and their apparent meaning. This part of the course is an attempt to train the candidate to think theologically, and to go on doing so throughout his ministry. All through this process, a man's faith is increasingly tested as he sees more clearly the implications of what at first he had only dimly seen or lightly grasped. Behind it all is the question of the relationship of God with man, the ways in which God has made known what that relationship is and shall be, and the ways in which he acts in the world. Thus the study of doctrine is a growth in sensitivity to the activity and presence of God rather than the learning of dogmatic assertions.

The relevance of scripture and Christian doctrine to human living is seen in the study of history and ethics. Personal morals and inter-personal relations and community problems are a field for theological thinking. A study of Church history is necessary because the Church of today is the product of its past, and those who serve and lead the Church need to understand what lies behind its structure and its divisions. Those who lead its worship need to understand why that worship is set in its present forms and so to grasp the theology which is expressed in the services of the Church. Personal moral problems cannot be isolated from the will of God. Thus the study of ethics and of moral theology is the beginning of a life-long process of thinking theologically about individual and corporate action in the world. Here again the faith of the student is tested as he sees the consequences of what he believes about the ultimate meaning of life on the situations that face men day by day. In particular, history (including Church history) and sociology give opportunity for a study of human community, its strengths and weaknesses and the root causes of conflict and the grounds of harmony. In all this he learns to discern the activity of God in the affairs of men. He learns to note when the Church has resisted the guidance of God and to see the consequences in its life and witness. He will study the lives of some of the great leaders in Church and State, learning from them how God used them to effect a particular part of his will at some moment of human history. In this he will learn to recognise some of the unchanging characteristics of Christian leadership.

There is at each theological college a certain amount of direct pastoral training, the equipping of the student with the skills later needed for his ministry. Of necessity this is introductory, as most of those skills have to be learned on the job. Basic training in Sunday School and Day School teaching methods, in the general principles of hospital and sick visiting, parish administration and allied topics will be given. There may be opportunity to do theological thinking about family, social and marital problems. There will be opportunity to visit psychiatric and other hospitals and to look at the question of the breakdown of body and of personality in the light of the gospel of Christ, who came to make men free and whole. There are no easy answers to the many questions which are raised in this way, but the student is learning sensitivity to the needs and frailty of men as he tries to see how God's grace can be, and is, brought to bear through love and prayer on the situations he meets. Some of these situations will prove to be a further testing of the faith of the student and so are occasions for helping him to be more ready for his work as a priest. In addition to contact with local parishes, where some insight can be gained into the aims and methods of parochial activities, there is usually a chance to make an extended visit to a parish as a corporate college activity during a vacation. Both in these parochial contacts and through the corporate worship in the college chapel, the student gains some of the skills needed (and learns some of the pitfalls which can occur) in the conduct of worship. Many of the skills have to be learned after ordination, and it is not possible to have more than theoretical knowledge about spiritual direction and personal counselling in advance.

More and more Colleges, however, arrange that their students shall have an extensive placement in a parish, and competence must be shown by each student not only in the academic field but also in pastoral studies, and in the theological understanding of what goes on in a parish. In addition, several Colleges help to train students who belong to other denominations in the Church and some are clearly ecumenical. In all these ways the student of today is given a far wider vision and fuller preparation for ministry than was possible previously.

The corporate, residential nature of most of the training leads to an understanding of community and of the forces and tensions which operate in groups of people. Even the evident continuity of a body of people, and the identity of the college, in which one-third of the members change annually, gives some insight into the cohesive forces which can operate in society. In an age of great mobility, such as that in which we now live, this insight is of great value. The part played by corporate worship in moulding the community and giving it unity and the power of continuity is experienced at first hand. There are opportunities for experiment in worship which are not available in normal parish life, so the student is able to reflect theologically about what is happening when corporate worship takes place.

During the whole period of his college training, the student has time and the opportunity to grow in the practice of private prayer and to lay foundations on which his life of prayer as a priest can be built. The sense of trust among members of a college, and between them and the staff, makes possible a discussion of method and sharing of experience in prayer which is likely to be something wholly new to the student. He can relate his study of theology to his personal prayer, linking both with his growing insights into the ways of God and the needs of men. It is this power to relate prayer and thinking theologically, rather than the ability to supply the answers to technical questions, which lies at the heart of training for priesthood in a theological college.

4

ORDINATION

THE choice of a parish where an ordination candidate first serves is partly his own, partly that of his sponsoring bishop and partly that of the Principal of his theological college who is inundated with requests for help from former members of the college. Since the work of a priest has to be learned in the doing of it, however well prepared the college may make him, the ordination candidate is encouraged to go to a parish where the incumbent will help him most rather than to a parish where the need for an extra ordained man is greatest. Vicars who understand how young curates feel in success and failure, who help them to order their lives and to grow in prayer, and who are glad to commend their services to another priest just when they are most useful to themselves, these training priests render valuable service to the Church. Relations between curates and vicars change each generation, and the fact that it is not uncommon for a young vicar to have an older curate accentuates the change. The vicar who has discovered for himself that priesthood is a way of life into which one grows, and a relationship with others (inside and outside the organised Church) which depends at least as much on a priest's character and role as it does on his skills, is the kind of man who will help the newly ordained grow into priesthood. They must be able to talk without reserve, to give and accept criticism, to pray and learn together how God is seeking to be served and how the presence of Christ is to be made known in the world. If the ordination candidate is married, his vicar will be understanding enough to know that his home is part of his life and not just the place where he lives.

When the preliminaries of the General Ordination Examination are over, arrangements made with the vicar of his parish-to-be and the bishop of the diocese is satisfied that all is well, having received Letters Testimonial and made a public announcement of the candidate's forthcoming ordination so that the people of his home parish may tell him of any possible impediment, then the candidate is invited to spend two or three days in retreat immediately before the ordination. Some experienced priest leads this retreat which gives the candidate that opportunity for recollectedness which helps him to enter fully into the Ordination Service.

Under the present system in the Church of England, and throughout the Anglican Communion, the candidate is ordered as a deacon and serves in that order for about a year before being ordained priest. The service for ordering deacons and ordaining priests is commonly conducted as one service, which makes diaconate appear as a stepping-stone to priesthood. Both are aspects of ministry and each represents the Church as the Body of Christ in whom priesthood and service reside and from whom they derive. There is an ambivalence to be found in our present system. The Ordinal says that a sermon shall be preached declaring how necessary is the order of deacon in one case, and the order of priest in the other, in the Church. Again, the parish to which a deacon goes sees him as a curate who is able to do most things but not quite everything; in a year's time he will be fully qualified. For the man himself, his ordering as a deacon makes him 'The Reverend . . .' and he begins to wear a clerical collar as the uniform of his office; for him and for his family this is a major break with his lay status in the past. Yet it is to the office and work of a priest that he is called; he is looking forward to the day when he will celebrate the Holy Communion for the first time and it is the jubilee of ordination to priesthood that many priests keep with joyful thanksgiving to God. Thus on the one hand, ordination to priesthood is the climax of a long process and the beginning of a life in new relationship with Christ's Church; on the other hand, clerical life begins on being made deacon to which an extra dimension is added after twelve months. It is the significance of the office of deacon which is lost more than that of priest. So long as diaconate is seen as a period of training in ecclesiactical administration and a necessary stepping-stone to priesthood, and so long as the ordination services remain conflated, this ambivalence will continue.

After a year in the parish where he has shared in leading worship, assisted in ministering Holy Communion, visited people in their homes and in hospital and discovered the value of the daily office not only as an expression of the ongoing prayer of the Church but as a ministry of intercession for the Church in the parish and beyond, the would-be priest looks forward to the day of his ordination. During this year he is learning from his involvement in pastoral ministry and his relationship with the vicar what the work of a priest, to which he believes himself called and to which his training has been directed, really is. There will have been some assessment of his readiness by the bishop's examining chaplains; there will have been a report from his vicar to the bishop; there will be a few days spent in retreat immediately before the ordination; there will be a talk with the bishop who is to have the privilege of ordaining him. He will have wrestled with himself until he is satisfied that his growing awareness of unworthiness is not to be confused with a sense of doubt as to whether God is calling him to priesthood.

The ordination is in the context of Holy Communion, itself a ministry of word and sacrament. The priesthood we share is priesthood in the Body of Christ who is the only true priest. Our offering of ourselves is of ourselves in him and of himself in us. Almost the first act of the priest after being ordained is to confess, with the Church, his sins and receive the word of absolution and then to hold out his hands to receive the Bread of Life. He is commissioned to declare that word and to offer that bread to others but first he identifies himself with those whom he is called to serve.

The Ministry of the Word at the ordination, both in the Book of Common Prayer and The Alternative Service Book 1980, is of pastoral care. The Epistle speaks of the variety of God's gifts, the way they should be used and the end to which they are directed. The Gospel is equally pastoral. The bishop's charge which follows speaks of the quality of life and devotion to duty required of the pastor. 'You are to be messengers, watchmen, and stewards of the Lord; you are to teach and to admonish, to feed and to provide for the Lord's family, to search for his children in the wilderness of this world's temptations and to guide them through its confusions, so that they may be saved through Christ for ever.' The resources available to the priest are the scriptures to inform his words, and the Holy Spirit to sanctify his life. Nothing is said of priestly privilege; much is said of pastoral responsibility. The questions that are put by the bishop relate first to a belief that this is a call from God to serve him as a priest in his Church. Reliance on the sufficiency of scripture, diligence in prayer and study, faithfulness in ministry, loyalty to the Church and a readiness to frame his personal and home life according to the way of Christ, are the substance of the remaining questions. The prayers of the people are focused in the words of the ancient hymn 'Come, Holy Ghost, our souls inspire', followed by the bishop's prayer of thanksgiving to God for calling those to be ordained to share in the ministry entrusted to the Church. The glory of God and the building up of the Church through pastoral care, 'that the world may come to know your glory and your love,' remain the theme of thanksgiving and of prayer.

The moment of ordination comes when the candidate kneels before the bishop, who lays his hands on his head; in this action other priests present are invited to join. This joint action did not take place when he was ordered deacon; on that occasion the bishop alone laid on his hands. The words of ordination are spoken by the bishop alone, for he is in this the spokesman of the Church. In the Book of Common Prayer the words spell out the duties of the priest. 'Receive the Holy Ghost for the office and work of a Priest in the Church of God, now committed unto thee by the imposition of our hands.Whose sins thou dost forgive, they are forgiven; and whose sins thou dost retain, they are retained.

And be thou a faithful dispenser of the Word of God and of his holy Sacraments; In the name of the Father, and of the Son, and of the Holy Ghost. Amen.' This form of words is different from those used when he was made a deacon. Then he was told 'Take thou authority to execute the office of a Deacon in the Church of God . . .' In The Alternative Service Book, the form of words is the same for each office. 'Send down the Holy Spirit upon your servant N. for the office and work of a priest (deacon) in your Church.' The duties of the office of priest are spelled out in the prayer which follows, to watch over those committed to his care, 'to absolve and bless them in your name, and to proclaim the gospel of your salvation. As you have called them to your service, make them worthy of their calling.' The Episcopal Church in the United States of America is equally definite in the prayer used 'Therefore, Father, through Jesus Christ your Son, give your Holy Spirit to N; fill him with grace and power, and make him a priest in your Church.'

While the bishop alone has through his consecration the responsibility of ordaining priests, the action of other priests present sharing in the laying on of hands makes clear that priesthood derives from the Church as a corporate entity. A priest is incorporated into the ordained priesthood which he receives. The priesthood he receives is likewise a commission to act as representative and spokesman of the Church, to the world and to the Church itself, and not an office which can be exercised independently of the Church. His priesthood is of the Church of God, not of any one part of it only. This is what the bishop believes God intends to convey and that to which the candidate is called; this is what the candidate believes God is giving him. The grace of God which enables him to exercise that priesthood he may reject; the responsibility to exercise it he believes to be part of the call of God who is unchanging in his will and in his power.

The experience of thousand upon thousand of those ordained priest is that something happened which transcended the realm of earthly things, something belonging to the realm of the eternal.

This experience does not rest on any feeling at the moment, vivid though that may have been, but on the meaning and context and intentions of the service as a whole and of those taking part. The words might demand qualification, but there is the conviction that 'God did something'. Similar words might be used at a baptism or a wedding or a Communion. Visible things and actions and audible words reach out beyond the realm of space and time and in their totality are charged with divine significance, and by them the divine will is done and the grace of God realised and received.

To describe this action of God in terms of imparting some indelible character to the man who is ordained priest is quite inadequate. The whole Church receives a new member of the ordained priesthood, who receives his priesthood from God through the Church. Thus God acts upon the Church, and not only upon the man. The bishop also receives a new degree of pastoral responsibility as well as being the spokesman and agent from whom pastoral responsibility is committed to the priest. There is giving and receiving by bishop, priest, fellow-priests and the Church as a whole; the grace of God is operative in all these relationships. The same sort of complex pattern is seen in baptism in which God gives new responsibility to the Church through the act by which the baptised person receives a new relationship to the Church.

When the act of ordination is complete, the Communion Service continues. All that has been done, and all that has led up to this time, is linked with the self-offering of Christ for men and to men. The newly ordained priest is able to see this Communion as his preparation for celebrating the Holy Communion for the first time himself. For this reason, if for no other, it is much to be desired that his first Communion as celebrating priest should not be long delayed and certainly it should be the next one at which he is present. In the course of a long ministry, he will celebrate the Holy Communion many thousand times. The spiritual danger of doing this unprepared, or at least inadequately prepared, will always be with him. The practice of using one Communion as preparation for the next, consciously and deliberately, may help him face this danger. The memory of his ordination, at which he received Communion, as both a preparation and commissioning for the first Communion he should celebrate, may help him all the more. This does not excuse him from other preparation before he celebrates, but rather helps him to do so. On the eve of the anniversary of his ordination as a priest he does well to set time aside to read again the whole ordination service as an extended meditation. This will deepen his penitence and enrich his thanksgiving for the grace of God extended to him, and refresh his desire so to be used by God that his grace may be received by others also.

5

SUNDAY SERVICES

APART from special occasions like baptisms, weddings and funerals it is at Sunday services that members of the general public are most likely to see and hear a priest. They would consider that he was ordained to take services and that this was his primary work. Whether they understood the purpose of public worship or not, their estimation of a priest would be closely linked with whether, in their opinion, he took a service well or badly. Their standards of good and bad may be their own, but they are likely to be to the point. They want a service to be intelligible, reverent and not too long. The point at which a service becomes too long is psychological and has little to do with the clock. If the attention of the worshipper is not held, and no awareness of God is communicated, the service very quickly becomes too long. To be intelligible does not only mean that the words of the sermon can be understood; it includes such simple things as being audible, and having pauses to allow the meaning of one sentence to be grasped before the next is said. Reverence communicates an awareness of God and is one of those intangibles to which the occasional worshipper is more sensitive than many clergymen give him credit for. But it is not only the priest who is being judged. In church he is seen as the man of God, and the relevance of Christ and the love of God for man are equally under judgement.

However simple and however small the number of people present, a church service is essentially formal. It is something which is being offered to God in a special place, in a special period of time, and only the best will suffice. The place itself has been set aside for the purpose, intended to be the setting for divine worship. Everything connected with the place should be directed to that end and, in the words of the 1662 rubric about bread for

35

the Communion, 'should be the best that conveniently may be gotten'. Limitations of money clearly mean that the most expensive is not always the most convenient, quite apart from whether it is the best. There is, however, no excuse for the second or third best when the best is available; nor is it worthy of the God to whom worship is offered not to care for the tidiness and cleanliness of a church. Careful attention to detail need not be fussiness, but can prevent small things from distracting the worshipper's attention. When there is to be a visit by the Mayor, or when the bishop comes to a parish, there is often a general clean-and-tidy; the churchyard looks attractive, there are no faded flowers in church, cobwebs are removed from windows, the eagle is polished and the whole place looks immaculate. If such trouble is taken for the visit of a bishop or a mayor, how much more should it not continually be taken for the worship of God. The experience of having a service televised from a parish church is a valuable lesson in attention to detail. The movement of the choir in step, the absence of obstacles to their progress, small matters of symmetry, the readiness of books open at the right place may seem very little things. If all choirboys and men had markers in their psalters before the service began, much distraction from attention to the lessons at Evensong would be avoided. These and many other details aid or hinder the total offering of worship.

A church service, as an offering to God, requires careful preparation. It may not be necessary for the whole service to be rehearsed, but those who share any part in its leadership should know in advance what they and others are to do. This means planning between the vicar, any curate or reader, the organist and choirmaster, the wardens and others. However much the incumbent may delegate his final responsibility for the music that is played and the hymns that are sung, these have their part in the total act of worship; they should relate to other things that are to be done, to the theme of the lessons and of the sermon. The readings should be studied in advance and if they are to be read by members of the congregation it may be wise to have a rehearsal.

If the service were broadcast, the readers would expect it. The point at which the reader of a lesson moves from his seat, the way he approaches the lectern, the opening of the bible at the right place and the manner of announcing the reading need planning if not rehearsing. The intercessions at a Communion Service, or the occasional prayers at Morning Prayer or Evensong, need to be planned as to their number, length and matter. When leading the intercessions, either at Holy Communion, or at Morning or Evening Prayer, it is most important that it is clear that the prayer is addressed to God; it is not a homily addressed to the congregation, even if it ends with 'Lord, in your mercy hear our prayer.'

The priest is the leader of worship and it is his responsibility to see that the worship offered is worthy to be offered. He must have in mind the people who share with him the conduct of the service and the congregation which is likely to be present. He has the latter in mind not because the service is a means of educating them but because he should enable the congregation to share in the offering of the worship. An interesting dilemma can face the priest here. Many services are activities of the Church; that is to say, it is assumed in the very structure of the service that those who are present are fellow-members of a believing community. Yet such services may be attended by people who are unbelievers or at least doubters, as well as by visitors who are unknown to the local church and who may belong to a church elsewhere. There is a delicate balance between interrupting the sequence of the service to ensure that these people are involved and carrying on as though they were not there, thus assuming that they are but watching what others are doing. There is generally too little distinction between services where the company of believers meets to offer prayer and praise, and services where the faith is declared to the world and at which those outside the regular worshipping company are invited and encouraged to take part in some act of worship. This applies on formal occasions when the Mayor and Town Councillors attend a fully choral Matins, and also in a growing number of parishes where the only service in the morning is a Parish Communion. It is very questionable whether the latter is the best, or even a right, medium for evangelistic outreach.

As leader of the worship of the Church, the priest should make as clear as possible what is being done. He does this both by his planning in advance and by his actions and manner at the time. Arriving in ample time to compose his mind and say a preparatory prayer before robing for the service will help both him and the people. Country clergy who serve several churches and are obliged to celebrate two or three Parish Communions on a Sunday morning suffer from a severe handicap here. It is hard to be calm and collected when one has had to drive fast from one village church in order to arrive at the next even five minutes before a Communion service is due to begin. Reverence and haste are uneasy bedfellows. Before the service, then, the priest will pray that all that shall be done may be to the greater glory of God and to the revealing of that glory to men; he will pray that every word and action of his own may be to that end; he will thank God for the privilege given to him in celebrating the Holy Communion and leading the worship of the church. If he does this in his cassock at the communion rail, it will be much easier for him to teach the people whose worship he leads to prepare their own hearts and minds through prayer for worship. Such organ music as may be played during the few minutes before the service should be subdued enough to allow composure and prayer to be possible. The priest then returns to the vestry to robe, says a vestry prayer with choir and servers, and they all process into church so that the service may begin at the time when it is stated it shall begin. In an age when television programmes, football matches and school periods are expected to begin on time, even human considerations demand that a service should start at the appointed time. At a said celebration, the priest can have entered and be standing in silent prayer before the altar until the clock strikes eight (or whatever the hour may be).

The parish priest has a great advantage over any visiting

minister, whether bishop or reader, in that he can consult with his people and agree with them matters of procedure like standing and kneeling, the places where they join in, the need or otherwise of announcing hymns and so on. Over-familiarity may breed a dullness of spirit at a service, but the distractions of not being sure what to do are a greater hindrance to good devotion. Thus if a service of Holy Communion is said, it is possible immediately before the Collect to remind the people what Sunday it is for which the Collect, Epistle and Gospel are appointed. At a sung service this is less convenient, but worshippers will be able to concentrate better if some notice were given just before the service; this is probably the best time to give out notices in any case. While clarity is important at all times, it is especially so in respect of those parts of the service which are proper to the Sunday, particularly the proper prefaces which break the familiar sequence of the ordinary preface. The priest does well to remember that for a congregation to change posture from standing to kneeling, or even sitting to standing, takes time; it severely disrupts attentiveness if one is still fumbling with a hassock when a prayer has begun. (Familiar danger points at a Communion according to the A.S.B. are after a sung Gloria, if the congregation is expected to kneel for the Collect, and after the Sanctus; and after the Creed at Morning or Evening Prayer.) In the light of all the options in respect of standing or kneeling, singing or speaking, and so on, it is time well spent to have a clear understanding with the organist, curate or reader, and with the congregation as a whole, just how things shall be done. Uniformity between one congregation and another may not be obtainable or right, but those who come regularly to the same church look for an established pattern of procedure.

It would be beyond the province of this book to treat the matter and manner of preaching at any length. A point which was raised earlier, however, arises here. Does the nature of the service assume that it is being offered by a believing community? The Holy Communion service does make this assumption, and the sermon should be prepared and delivered with this in mind. The priest is speaking to the gathered Church. In most parish churches, unless deliberate steps are taken to draw in visitors, the same will apply at Evensong. The priest can assume a willingness to learn, a readiness to act and a desire to pray better, and can teach and preach accordingly. The same assumption cannot be made at a parade service of any kind, and on such occasions it is right to speak about the Christian faith in more general terms and to explain what it means. There are some churches which have become known as centres of evangelism; in such churches the distinction between preaching to the company of the faithful and preaching with intent to evangelise is at its most clear. A sermon to either kind of congregation, however, will be prepared with meticulous care if it is to be fit to be part of an act of worship. Many priests find that the shorter the sermon, the longer the preparation.

The nature of the congregation will determine not only the type of preaching but the content of the intercession. This is one point in the service where the company of faithful people can express its concern about immediate personal needs and also look outside itself to the needs of the world at large and the universal Church. Thus it is right to pray for the Church overseas using, probably, the Anglican Cycle of Prayer; it is equally right to pray by name for members of the parish who are to be baptised or married or who are being prepared for confirmation. It is right to remember victims of plague in India, and also to remember by name the local sick persons who are known to members of the congregation. The wise parish priest will encourage his parishioners to provide material for such prayer, perhaps by having a box where requests may be placed which will be cleared by Saturday evening each week. Once the idea has been grasped there is no question as to its value; if the Parochial Church Council can go together on a residential week-end, the idea can easily be grasped. In a small parish, the names of the departed can be remembered on the anniversary of their death (relatives having been told in advance); in a large parish, the names of those who died in the preceding week can be remembered. Other members of the Christian family, whose names are in the list of universally acknowledged saints, are remembered when their days come round. The balance between the world-wide and the local can and should appear in the intercession at the Holy Communion which is a local expression of that which extends throughout time and space.

Since it is easier to revise a liturgy than to rebuild a church, or even to persuade the congregation that the furniture should be radically rearranged, it is common practice for the Ministry of the Word (in the ASB) to be taken by the priest from his stall near the chancel step. Quite apart from any literal obedience to the rubrics, it is far less convenient to do this with the 1662 service. Using the ASB, the movement from priest's stall to the altar can take place either after the intercession, or after the Pax. What is difficult is to kneel to confess one's sins facing west behind a table which is on the high side and then to pronounce the absolution over the altar. (With a nave altar there is little or no problem.) The problem continues when one kneels again for the prayer of humble access. The difficulty is solved if the priest moves from his stall after the intercession, stopping before the altar for the whole of the preparation of the people. Indeed, there is some symbolism of his oneness with the rest of the Church whose Eucharist he is leading by his position in confession and prayer of humble access; there is also corresponding symbolism in his facing the people for the absolution, comfortable words and the Pax. He can then move behind the altar, if westward-facing position is used, at the offertory.

With the rapid revision of liturgies for experimental use both in England and in other parts of the Anglican Communion, one cannot do more at this point than indicate some general principles which the priest will follow. From the start of the Thanksgiving to the end, the priest is exercising a particular form of leadership; he invites the people to lift up their hearts in thanksgiving; in the preface he declares the grounds of that thanksgiving, and so invites the people to join with the heavenly host in praise to God for his mighty acts for our redemption. He is leading the Church in its remembrance of Christ in the way he asked that he should be remembered. Here is no drama which the priest enacts, but a pilgrimage which he leads to the upper room, to the cross, and beyond to the realised presence of the risen and ascended Christ. On Christ's behalf in sacramental form, he leads the members of Christ to a renewed assurance that the life given for them is given to them. It would destroy the reality of the mystery to seek to define at what point and in what manner God acts in this, or to circumscribe his action to make it dependent upon the priest; but that he does so act is the experience of countless faithful Christian souls. That God in some way uses the priests whom he has called to convey to others not only pardon and cleansing, but new life in Christ, is also a fact of experience; and the priest so used knows only too well that neither the pardon nor the new life were his own to give but Christ's, and that he himself is in as much need of them as the people to whom he ministers.

Details of action and ceremony will vary from priest to priest, and from church to church. There is no one right manner of stance or action or speech which makes all other ways wrong. Clarity of voice, simplicity and visibility of action, and reverence in manner, will control the priest in all things. The invitation to 'draw near' will be given with gentle authority, and the words of administration spoken individually with concern and love for a fellow-member of the Body of Christ. Who knows in this uncertain world and transitory life for which person kneeling at the rail this may be his 'last Communion'? The opportunity given in The Alternative Service Book for the communicant to say 'Amen' makes the words of administration easier to make personal. The custom of bringing infants and, indeed, of children coming on their own to the communion rail to receive a blessing is now widespread. The celebrant who administers the bread can place his hand on the head of each such child and say 'The Lord bless you and keep you. Amen'. There is absolutely no need for a second blessing from whoever ministers the cup.

When all communicants have received the bread and wine the ablutions follow as unobtrusively as possible. The priest concludes the service by leading the prayer of thanksgiving or the short prayer of self-offering in the service of God and in the power of the Spirit, which all join in saying. The blessing or dismissal follows, and the priest and any assistants return to the vestry. The informal word with individual worshippers as they leave the church is but an extension of the more formal dismissal; to see it as such is some compensation for the delay in being able to say a thanksgiving for the privilege of celebrating that Holy Communion.

The same principles of preparedness, of clarity of speech and attention to detail, of concern for the worshippers and of reverence towards God to whom the worship is offered, will apply in the conduct of all other Sunday services of the church. The prevalence of the Parish Communion as the principal, if not only, service on a Sunday morning and the decline of Evensong which is widespread, make the need for non-liturgical services far greater than formerly. Non-liturgical is, of course, a false description. Freedom to vary the form and adapt the style of language to suit the particular congregation and circumstance is demanded. Many such services—family services, children's services, variations on 'Songs of Praise' or of the Nine Lessons and Carols—are published and still more are individually devised. Even if the service may be adapted at the time (depending upon the proportion of adults and children, for instance) it needs to be carefully planned and variations thought out in advance. Strictly speaking, all such services come under the provisions of Canon B 5 and in cases of genuine doubt the matter may be referred to the bishop; it is unlikely that most bishops would welcome having to approve the form of the family service on Mothering Sunday for every parish in a diocese, or read the text of every nativity play. What Canons B 4 and B 5 do is to recognise the need for services to meet circumstances for which no provision is made in the Book of Common Prayer or The Alternative Service Book.

Services for such special occasions should not be watered-down versions of Matins or Evensong. It is by no means obvious that the congregation would be ready to start with a cheerful hymn and pass·immediately to the confession of sin; indeed, it is doubtful whether it is right to expect a congregation of visitors to confess their sins without due preparation. It is not necessary that there be two lessons, one from the Old and one from the New Testament; nor is it self-evident that it is right always to say the Creed. Assumptions which are justified when the local church is gathered do not apply, and the whole service needs to be planned without such preconceptions. It is important that such a service be in the language and thought-form of the people who will be present. It is good if appropriate parts can be read or led by members of the congregation, after due warning and rehearsal. It is much to be desired that an order of service should be printed or duplicated and every member of the congregation provided with a copy. Directions for sitting, standing or kneeling should be absolutely clear, and ample time allowed for any change of position or for the place to be found when a hymn is announced. The people can only be led from where they are already, so that generous use of familiar hymns and prayers is both kind and wise; hymn tunes that are unfamiliar or pitched too high, or both, destroy both interest and concentration.

The part of the priest, both in the planning and the conduct of such services, is to lead the people from where they are in their thinking and living to an awareness of the presence and will and power of God; the service, and any sermon which forms part of it, will be designed to help the people to respond to God from their situation and in it. Whilst it is right to withdraw from the pressure of activity to see that activity in the light of the love and power of God, the service must point back to the situation in which the participants live. It is the task of the priest to try to see all things and people in their relation to God, actual and potential.

He cannot do this if he is only concerned about God and does not consider the people. In fact it will not be God, revealed in Christ, that he will be concerned about if he does not consider the people. It follows that the service must not be an escape from the world of sin and activity to a haven of pardon and peace which can only be found in a church. The traffic sign 'No through road— To Church only' may be necessary physically; it should never apply to what goes on in a church. Thus, as a small illustration, however right it is to bless the Mayor and Town Councillors or the local Young Farmers, it is as important to bid them to go forth in peace . . . rejoicing in the power of the Spirit.

The priest will never know the effect of such a service, except in so far as the enthusiasm for the next one is some indication. He is concerned about the honour of God and if he can help a group of people to give God a little of the honour due to him, that is his task. He is concerned that the Kingship of God shall be acknowledged on earth and if the service, and any sermon he may preach, makes the Kingship desired and accepted, that is his task. He is concerned that the Church, as the Body of Christ, shall be strengthened for service and if any individual is drawn to take his rightful place in the Church as a result of worshipping in this way, that is good.

When the Sunday services are over, the priest will take occasion in his private prayer to think back on them. There will be ground for thanksgiving for his privilege to serve God and the people in this way, and many special thanksgivings because of the response there has been. There will be ground for some disappointment because of the lack of greater response. There will be ground for penitence for many imperfections. There will be ground for prayer that those who shared in the worship may be renewed in spirit. Just as he himself, with all his weaknesses and faults, is taken and used by God to lead the people to find means of grace so he prays that the worship that he led, with all its faults, may be woven into the pattern of God's plan for man's salvation.

6

BAPTISM AND CONFIRMATION

THE parish priest is bound to spend considerable time in touch with families in connection with baptisms, though the proportion of infants born in England who are baptised in the Church of England has dropped, especially in the big cities. If the recommendations of the Archbishops' Commission on Christian Initiation had been accepted and put into effect, there might have been fewer infant baptisms, but more time would have been given to explaining to parents and congregations the meaning of baptism. At present, the debate on indiscriminate baptism continues; the practice also continues, to the discomfort of clergy and to the relief of nominal Christians. One point on which differences arise is that the clergy want the baptism to take place at a main Sunday service, to make clear that the child is being incorporated into the visible fellowship of the Church; the parents want the service to be as domestic as possible, to emphasise the personal and family aspect. Again, the parents choose the godparents for largely family reasons; the clergy are anxious that godparents should be committed churchmen. If the priest compromises again and again, he brings the sacrament of baptism into disrepute. On the other hand, if he is too outspoken about the lack of church-going by the parents and godparents, he receives publicity as one who refuses baptism to an innocent child.

Baptism is initiation into the Church as a visible society. As the Body of Christ, the Church shares in a peculiar way the sonship of Christ; the child who becomes a member of Christ can address God as Father in a new and particular way. There is an important family element in baptism, and that family is represented locally by the gathered congregation. There is an important family

47

responsibility in baptism, for when a child is born into a family all the members of that family have a responsibility to the child. The parish priest, therefore, should regularly remind the whole congregation of its duty to the newly made member of the Church. It just is not realistic to complain that godparents neglect their duties, and to leave it at that. Plain and straightforward teaching and preaching about the Fatherhood of God, about the family character of the Church and of the mutual responsibilities of its members and about man's growth into Christ are an essential part of the work of the priest. This is more important today in a mobile society than in any previous age. The need to belong, which is an expression of man's basic need for significance and security, is a permanent need; but when domestic home-life is less secure and change of address more frequent, the need to belong is felt more strongly. The task of the priest in fostering the sense of belonging within the Family of God and its visible expression in the Church is a task of the highest social importance, quite apart from its theological significance.

The local church, as the visible expression of the family of God in a place, is not a human club but part of a divine community. The primary agent in baptism is not the infant who joins the community, nor the godparents who make promises which are accepted by the Church on the child's behalf, but God. It is God who declares the child to be his own, for he alone can make the child his own; through the agency of his representative, he places the child in the context of the earthly part of the divine society. In the case of infant baptism, the child has no choice; but in the case of human birth, the child has no choice either. It is through the will of the parents that a child is born. It is through the will of God the Father that a child can be adopted into that sonship which the Church shares through Christ. It is the will of God that all men should be saved and come to the knowledge of him in Christ. As the minister of baptism, the priest is helping forward the work of transforming what is into what ought to be by linking the earthly family with the family of God.

Even before any major reforms occur in the practice of the Church, there are several things that the priest can do to make baptism more nearly an expression of its true meaning. The first step is to explain to the congregation that just as a child cannot be received into the Church in the absence of the child itself, no more can the child be received in the absence of the Church. If there is to be genuine overlapping of the domestic family and the Church family, both must be present. The practical problems will vary from place to place. In a country parish, there will be little difficulty in having public baptism in the context of the Parish Communion on a Sunday, or at Morning or Evening Prayer. In a suburban parish with 50–100 or more baptisms a year, this would mean that at least on one Sunday a month there would be public baptism at a main Sunday service, which calls for quite a long-suffering congregation. So long as the fellowship of the Church and that of the domestic family genuinely overlap, it does not seem necessary for the whole church to be present at every baptism. In any case, the congregation is but one expression or embodiment locally of the Church Universal and there are few large parishes where the whole of that local embodiment is gathered at the same place at the same time. What does matter is that at every baptism service there shall be a genuine representation of the local church; and conversely that baptisms shall take place at such times that every member of the local church shall have occasion to be at some baptism. In this way, every new member will have been received by the congregation, adequately represented; also, every member of the congregation will have been put in mind of his part in receiving and supporting the new members.

The priest should impress on the congregation that responsibility for the new member continues at least until he is of age. The Sunday School or Children's Church looks to the Baptism Register to provide the names of its future members, and very likely birthday or baptism anniversary cards will be sent. Probably on the fourth birthday the card will include an invitation to join the Primary Sunday School. Preferably a visit will be made by a lay person (in addition to any visit by the priest) so that the invitation to the Primary Sunday School may be given in person and all explanations of time and place may be given. When the child does arrive at Sunday School, he should be positively welcomed by the rest of the Sunday School. Some form of Parent-Teachers Association will help the parents of the new scholar themselves to belong to the church which has a concern for their child. In a large parish the task of providing and sending birthday cards, and of arranging the visits to invite children to Sunday School, is demanding enough to require one person to make it his whole responsibility. This concern by the local church, with the parish priest in the closest touch, is far more practical than any attempt to prepare godparents before the service (and forget about them after it). In any case, godparents are increasingly inaccessible,[1] and to talk about preparing them is not being realistic.

However well the priest and his Church Council may agree on parochial policy and practice as regards infant baptism, the first intimation to the vicar will probably be a young mother, complete with pram, arriving at the vicarage asking for John or Mary to be christened on Sunday week if possible at 3 p.m. It is from this point that the parish priest starts, except in those parts of the north of England where the first contact is a request to be churched as the mother wants to go out. The Churching of Women is robbed of its true meaning of thanksgiving if the mother alone is present; the father has at least as much ground to thank God for the safe delivery as his wife has. If possible, the parish priest will explain that he will be only too happy to come to the house when the father is home from work and that then they can all thank God for the birth of the child and ask for God's guidance to them as parents and for his blessing on their home. If this can

[1] In my last two years 1964–65 at Allerton, a residential suburb of Liverpool, there were 159 baptisms. These children had 480 godparents of whom 96 lived in the parish and 384 lived outside the parish. Preparation of godparents is just not practical.

be arranged, the priest will visit the home and, after explaining to both parents what he hopes to do and for what they are giving thanks to God, will go with them to where the new baby is sleeping and there lead their prayers. Where there are already other children in the family, they should be invited to join. In The Alternative Service Book an Order of Thanksgiving for the Birth of a Child has been produced, and also a Thanksgiving after Adoption, which may be used either in church or in the home. God is praised for the wonder and joy of creation, and thanked for the life of the newly born child, for the safe delivery and for the privilege of parenthood. Prayer is made by the parents that they may be trustworthy, patient and understanding. There is a reading from the Gospel according to St Mark (10. 13-16) after which 'the minister may give a copy of one of the gospels to the parents.' The Lord's Prayer, linking the domestic family with the family of God, is said by all and a blessing given.

The details relating to baptism can then be discussed and the meaning of baptism as incorporation into the Church explained. The parents want the very best for their child; God wants the very best for the child also, and the knowledge of Christ and his love is part of this very best. The local congregation wants to share in giving the child a welcome as a new member of Christ, and so the baptism service concerns far more people than the parents, godparents and immediate relations. The priest can explain that a child learns at first largely by copying, and to see his parents praying will help him to pray more than anything else. If the parents say their prayers together in the child's presence as they have just done a few minutes ago, the child will grow up in an atmosphere of prayer; in addition their own thanksgiving and need for God's grace in the exercise of parenthood will be kept alive. The opportunity may also be taken to explain some points in the baptism service. It is not fair to complain that parents and godparents take solemn promises lightly unless those promises have been adequately explained. The chance to do this for god-parents is not easily found, but for the parents themselves it is.

When the service of baptism actually takes place, the priest can do much to emphasise its importance with dignity and with simplicity. The public character of the service is brought out more strongly if there is more than one child to be baptised, and if the service takes place in the context of Holy Communion or of Morning or Evening Prayer. If the order of the ASB is followed correctly the service will not begin at the font, but in the body of the church; the parents and sponsors affirm their own allegiance to Christ and their rejection of evil within the congregation. There is then a procession to the font, the priest leading the parents and sponsors. The water is blessed and the questions asked concerning the Christian profession in which the children are to be baptised and brought up. The congregation declare that they share the same faith by responding to 'This is the faith of the Church' in saying 'This is our faith. We believe and trust in one God, Father, Son and Holy Spirit.' In this way they identify themselves with the family of the child being baptised. Every member of the congregation should have a copy of the service so that all can join in the prayer for each child at the signing with the sign of the cross, the giving of the candle (if this is done) and the welcome into the Lord's family. In the Methodist Church, the congregation is asked whether it 'will endeavour so to maintain here a fellowship of worship and service in the Church that he may grow up in the knowledge and love of God and of His Son Jesus Christ our Lord', to which the reply is given 'We will, God being our helper'.[1] When the service is over, the priest will give to the parents a signed card in which the baptism is recorded and an empty space for the confirmation to be recorded when it takes place. The baptism register will, of course, be completed and signed.

If there is an Area Leader system working in the parish, the priest will have told the relevant Area Leader in advance about the baptism, so that local contact and offers to baby-sit may be

[1] *The Book of Offices* (Methodist Publishing House). Order of Service for the Baptism of Infants.

made. He will also send to the leader of the Primary Sunday School information about the baptism so that birthday cards may be sent on the correct date. In all this, the priest is acting as the leader of the congregation which is the local embodiment of the Church of God. Through baptism, God has given to the Church an added responsibility which rests primarily on the local congregation. In all his dealings with both the family and with the congregation the priest can make clear that it is God who acts in baptism. The event of birth and the gift of new life is brought into relation with God's will and love for the child and the family. In the divine encounter which takes place in baptism there can be glimpsed something of the continual divine action in the life of men who are called in Christ to be children of God.

The provision that is made in a parish for the children to grow in the faith and life of the Church varies widely. What is commonly called Voluntary Religious Education may cover anything from a well-ordered Sunday School or Children's Church to a group with little aim or purpose. The ordering of this work, which includes the general oversight of the syllabus and the finding, training and encouragement of teachers, is a task which the parish priest will find to be both exacting and rewarding. Asking for volunteers for this work is not the surest way to obtain the teachers that are wanted; asking particular people to fill a particular position in the Sunday School is more likely to produce the right results. It should not be assumed that once a Sunday School teacher, always a Sunday School teacher. The preparation of the teachers to teach and lead is as important as their preparation of the material for each week. Every diocese has an adviser who is ready to help the clergy in this task. The aim of Children's Church or Sunday School is not so much instruction in Christian doctrine as growth in the Christian family. For this reason as much involvement of the parents as possible is to be desired. The practice in parts of the Episcopal Church in the United States of keeping the children in church on two Sundays of the year and asking the parents to meet their children's teachers who would explain how and what their children were learning comes as a shock at first, but it certainly involves the parents.

If the parish is fortunate enough to have a Church School, an opportunity is given to the Church to exercise its ministry of teaching. The parish priest can share in that ministry and establish a link between the school and the worshipping community. He will know and be known by the children, lead their morning assembly and, in many cases, share some of the teaching of religious education. That he should be equipped and trained for this task is essential, and that he should be further trained to keep abreast of the changing pattern of education is equally important. In addition to his presence in the school during school hours, he will be on the Board of Governors (probably its chairman) and have opportunities to know the parents if there is a Parent-Teacher Association. This may also apply even if the school is a County School. In these ways, the priest is involved in the partnership of Church and State in education, and knowing the families is invaluable in his pastoral work. Children cannot be brought up to grow in the Christian family as something separate from their domestic earthly family, and preparation for confirmation which concentrates on the child and neglects the parents is doomed to continual disappointment.

Confirmation, as practised at present, has two distinct aspects. There is that of growing up in the family of God and the training to receive Holy Communion with understanding and faith. There is also that of renewing, or taking upon oneself, vows made in baptism which emphasises the element of personal commitment to Christ. Priests of a catholic persuasion see such value in the first element that they encourage candidates to be presented at an early age; priests of a more evangelical persuasion prefer to present candidates at a later age so that the commitment to Christ may be more mature. There is no happy mean and the report of the Archbishops' Commission on Christian Initiation recognised the point, recommending the separation of these two elements. The work of the priest remains the same, though divided in time. He will still prepare young people to understand the meaning of the Holy Communion and to take their full part in it, including the part of receiving. The first communion of those so prepared will be an event, not only for them but for the Church represented by the local congregation. If it is separated from confirmation, the bishop will normally celebrate and the whole worshipping community will be encouraged to be present. The priest will have explained to the Parochial Church Council the importance of the occasion and every member should be present as a matter of first priority. In other words, the preparation of the candidates is only one part of the priest's work; the preparation of the congregation to receive the candidates into the communicant fellowship of the Church is at least as great a part. In the United Reformed Church, the Church Meeting and Elders' Meeting discuss and approve candidates before they are confirmed or admitted to full membership; at the service the ministers and elders give to each candidate the right hand of fellowship. The same idea could be expressed in many ways and may be done at the social gathering after the service by a churchwarden or some other lay person giving a greeting or welcome to the new communicants.

The practice of having confirmation sponsors can easily be adapted if first Communion is separated from confirmation. There are some principles, proved in practice, which the priest is wise to recognise. The sponsors must be chosen by the priest, after consultation with any lay people (such as Bible Class Leaders) who may have a share in the training of the candidates and are responsible to the priest, acting as his link with the candidates until such time as they can act as sponsors to others. They must be of the same sex as the candidate, and probably not more than two years older so that they understand their way of thinking. The priest will train the sponsors in their task of support and encouragement before their introduction to the candidates, which will take place about half-way through the period of preparation. Under the present system of confirmation, the sponsors may stand behind the candidates as they come to kneel before the bishop and give him the name of the candidate. In a parish seriously affected by mobility, as in some city suburbs (and still more in America) it may be useful to have two sponsors to a group of six candidates to ensure continuity. They will act as helpers and leaders at any residential conferences, camps or meetings, and post-communion breakfasts.

The priest will find it valuable to invite the baptismal godparents to come to the confirmation or First Communion. The candidates can be asked to give to him the names and addresses of their godparents so that a duplicated, but personally signed, letter of invitation may be sent. Even those who live far away appreciate the invitation and many make the effort to come.[1] Still more valuable is a meeting of all the parents of the candidates some six weeks or so before the confirmation. A duplicated, but personally signed, invitation should be sent in good time asking that both parents should be present and requesting a reply. If numbers are sufficient, a bookstall can be arranged; books suitable for the parents as well as for the candidates should be provided. Some light refreshment puts people at their ease. The priest can then explain to the parents how Church and home can work together in the best interests of the children. He will explain something of the preparation he has been giving to the children in regard to prayer and worship, and concerning the standards, faith and practice of the Church; he can point out how necessary it is for the child that the standards, faith and practice of the home should be in harmony with those of the Church. He can explain to the parents something of the spiritual development of children and young people of the age of the candidates, and of their need for freedom and privacy of thought. He can explain what provision the Church makes for young people to exercise some freedom, away from both home and school; this gives him a

---

[1] In the last year in the parish for which I was responsible as parish priest there were 52 candidates presented with 108 surviving godparents, 98 of whom lived outside the parish, but more than half were present.

chance to outline the programme of the Church for young people. If the parents are not themselves communicants, training for this can be arranged and shyness in regard to this is reduced by finding others in the same situation.

It is an interesting commentary on our attitude to confirmation that in the occasional prayers in the 1928 Prayer Book, as in the Scottish and the American Prayer Books, the prayer under the heading Confirmation speaks only of the candidates and of what it is desired that God should do for them. If the Church is to be used by God as a channel of the Spirit and if part of the power of the Spirit is to be conveyed through the fellowship of the Church, then our prayers are needed not only for the candidates but for the Church into the full communicant membership of which they are to be admitted. The following prayer is one that the congregation may use.

O God, you have led your servants to share the divine life through the Communion of the Body and Blood of Christ, grant that our fellowship may be so strengthened by your Holy Spirit that we may be ready to receive them and welcome them; that both they and we may grow together in grace as we share our common life in you; through the same Jesus Christ our Lord. Amen.

In all his work in connection with baptism and confirmation, the priest is exercising his ministry in the Body of Christ to bring children to birth and growth within the Body and to lead the other members of the Body to accept them. He is bringing together what is, namely that John or Mary is the child of Mr and Mrs Smith, with what God desires, namely that John or Mary should come to know God as Father through Christ his son.

7

CHRISTIAN MARRIAGE AND CHURCH WEDDINGS

THE parish priest may expect, as a rough estimate, to conduct three weddings a year for every thousand people in his parish; but as a priest, his concern is with Christian marriage more than with church weddings. Christian marriage involves the union of man and woman with a loyalty and love, given and received without reserve and without limit. Such love derives from the love of God in Christ and also reflects Christ's love for mankind. The task of the priest is to help those who come, or may some day come to be married in church, to find in their marriage all the richness of joy which God has available for them. This task cannot be done if he waits till the couple ring the vicarage bell to put up the banns, though, in many cases, this will prove to be his starting-point. Preparation for marriage begins in infancy, for the experience of unconditional love in childhood is the best preparation for giving it in maturity. The priest will see to it that there is honest discussion about personal relationships in the church youth club with, possibly, the aid of a marriage guidance counsellor. Such discussion has little to do with sex instruction but has much to do with the dignity of man and relations between whole people. The priest will preach about the positive side of marriage as a laboratory of love, which is the gift of God, and not just negatively against divorce. He will speak openly about the virture of responsible parenthood rather than the vice of irresponsible love-making. Several matters of Christian concern close to the heart of the faith, such as acceptance and loyalty and forgiveness, are so much a part of marriage that they are natural subjects about which to preach. The priest will speak openly of home-making as a vocation from God to build a new family unit in fellowship with God in Christ.

Young couples who have neither heard a word of this preaching nor joined, either singly or together, in any youth club discussion will arrive at the vicarage to make arrangements for their wedding. They will be full of several fears: fear of the unknown parson, fear of the future generally, fear lest they will be rebuffed for asking for a church wedding when they do not belong and many other fears which make them all keyed up. The priest will do all in his power to put them at their ease and will give them all the time at his disposal, inviting them in and making them welcome. A sofa just large enough for two, and no larger, is an essential piece of equipment in a vicarage study! The priest will first discover whether the couple want to be married in his church, or just to put up the banns prior to marriage in another parish. Even in the latter case, he will not hurry them away but will patiently accept the information and satisfy himself that residence and any other requirement is all in order. It saves no end of time in the long run if the priest takes down the particulars himself, possibly with a running commentary as he asks the various questions. There is scope to talk about their jobs, about getting on with the parents and 'in-laws', about where they are going to live, about the girl going on working and the danger of getting used to two wages to feed two mouths, when someday there will be only one to feed three, and so on. This conversation can take place without having to look at them, which is an additional way of putting them at their ease. Given a little experience, the priest can talk quite naturally about white weddings and all for which they stand. He can very easily move from that to simpler matters like music and whether they will want the choir. Throughout the conversation he will address most of his remarks to the man. Quite apart from any psychological and emotional reasons, talking to the man emphasises the fact that a church wedding is not just the bride's concern. He may think it right to give them some literature, such as *The Threshold of Marriage* or the current

BMA booklet, *Getting Married* (which covers most topics from cookery to contraception). He will also fix a date about three or four weeks before the wedding when they will come again to go through the service so that they will know just what is going to happen on the day. When they have gone, he will add their names to his prayer list, thanking God for the privilege he is being given to open the eyes of two young people, whose love sees no further than each other, to the source of all their joy.

While the couple are answering questions about age and occupation and so on, the opportunity may well be taken to discover differences of religious persuasion which they may wish to discuss. The priest will be most careful to avoid giving the impression that he regards the wedding as a means of getting two new members. Naturally he would be delighted, but that is irrelevant. His task is to enable them to receive all that the God of love has available for them and wants them to have, and in some form he should say this to them in the simplest possible way. In fact, the number of young couples who begin to worship together after this initial talk is quite appreciable.

When the couple come again 'to go through the service', the priest may need to strike a slightly more definite note of authority, coupled with gentleness. After all, they do this once in a lifetime and he is quite likely to do his part a thousand or more times. He will ask them to sit on the sofa, the man having the girl on his left, and given them one copy of the service. If he knows the service by heart himself, the whole proceeding takes on a different character. The time spent in learning the baptism, wedding and funeral services by heart is repaid generously. Having put the couple at their ease, rechecked the particulars (there may have been a change of address, or the bridegroom's father may have died) and confirmed musical and other arrangements, the priest can leisurely bring out the meaning of the service. The introduction provides ample scope to discuss the social, family and personal sides of marriage. The description of marriage as a 'holy estate' and indeed the whole spirit of the service makes it clear that God is concerned about their whole life together to which the service leads. The priest may speak about the question 'Will you take N. to be your wife?', and point out that it does not ask 'Do you love her?' but 'Will you love her?'. There is all the difference in the world. The significance of the giving-away of the bride by her father can be explained. She joined her family as a gift from God twenty or so years ago; the father now passes her hand to the priest, who is acting in the name of God, so that she may join the bridegroom as a gift from God to create a new family. He then takes her as she is, with all her family background, her virtues and her faults, without any conditions attached, to love and to hold dear till death alone shall part them, and she takes him equally freely. If God meant this to be, and if their mutual giving and receiving is genuine, then something of more than earthly significance has happened. The ring will be an earthly sign of this, and the priest will explain how the ring is handed over, blessed and given to the bridegroom to put on the fourth finger of the bride's left hand. Under the discretion given to the minister to make minor variations, there is no reason why the bride should not say the same words 'I give you this ring . . .' (in the ASB) in those cases where each has a ring. The priest can explain just how the couple kneel for the declaration and the first blessing, pointing out that his clasping of their hands (and, maybe, wrapping the stole round them) signifies that the hand of God can and will hold them together in love.

The first half of the service comprises all that is needed for a legal marriage, so that it is possible for the registers to be signed at this point rather than in the vestry after the service. To do this has several advantages; it is much more expeditious, and enables the exit of the couple and families and friends at the end to be more dignified. There may be some anthem or organ voluntary while the registers are being signed. The priest is wise to ask the couple who the witnesses will be and, if they are not the two fathers, what their names and initials are; he has to send a copy to the

Registrar of Births, Marriages and Deaths at the end of the quarter, and some signatures are more legible than others.

The priest will then explain the second part of the service, pointing out when he gives his address and how they follow him up to the communion rail. The prayers which precede the Lord's Prayer give him a chance to discuss their own hopes for the guidance of God in their life together, the blessing of a family and the growth of their love. He may point out that the very first thing that they will do as man and wife is to pray together, and he can assure them that if they place themselves together daily in the hands of God they will be more able to follow his guidance and receive the blessings he has in store for them.

When the actual wedding-day comes, the couple will be far more at their ease and able to enter into the meaning of the service. The beginning of their courtship may have come about through some apparent chance, and their mutual attraction may have begun from a very earthly cause. Attraction has grown into love and the love which they pledge is a love which is of God; if they are held together by such love, they are held together by God, for God is love. It is for the priest to open their eyes to the meaning of the situation into which God has led them. This has little connection with those outward things which make up a 'lovely wedding', good though those things may be. It is quite likely the priest will be invited to the wedding reception. He must be consistent in practice and not give an opening for people to say he accepts some invitations but not others. The story of Cana in Galilee is not a precedent but may assure the priest that he is not doing wrong to accept.

As a priest he is concerned with their marriage and not only with the wedding service. If they move away to live, he should send a commendation to the vicar of the parish where their home will be; this is a practice much neglected. If they live in the parish where they are married, the priest will make a point of visiting them after about a month and will make a note to send them a card on their first anniversay. A newly married couple who come into the parish to live may be invited on a Sunday evening to meet two other newly married couples. It is easy to allow the claims of home to become all-absorbing and the priest can help a young couple in new surroundings to find friends and, in an increasingly mobile society, to act as friends to a more recently married couple. One of the stabilising factors which belongs to a less mobile society is that of being surrounded by friends and relations. Freedom to start one's married life in a new context carries with it the loss of this factor. The role of the Church as a welcoming and accepting society even at the earthly level is of great social value. Its strong familial structure counterbalances the absence of close earthly family groupings.

When children begin to arrive, the wise priest can help the young couple to adjust to their new relationships and responsibilities. The Christian Gospel has much to say about the balance of inclination and loyalties to family, friends and the world, of discipline and freedom. All these factors come into play in a new way when a young couple are responsible for bringing a new life into the world. God wants the child to have all the security and love that he has to give, and he wants the parents to have the joy of giving it. The priest who tries to see all things and people in their relationship to God can help the new parents find this joy.

If the Church believes that married couples are strengthened by worshipping together (quite apart from the primary purpose of worship which is to give God his due honour), then it is up to the Church to make this not only possible but convenient. Baby care and kindergarten care, Sunday Schools that coincide with family worship, and the welcoming of children at the communion rail for a blessing, are signs of a Church that cares. The priest will not only encourage these, but also see that parents who take advantage of nursery care are allowed and asked to take their share in providing it. But the priest's concern is not just to enable parents to come to church on a Sunday, but to help them live a whole life. A parochial baby-sitting club, organised on a co-operative basis, can be a valuable social service, especially in a new housing area. The need for this is greater in a society where young couples are far removed from grandparents, aunts and sisters.

The priest may arrange a periodic marriage reunion in some form or other, which need in no way be seen as a stunt. Of course it gives the vicar a chance to meet again couples he has married and for them to meet one another and exchange baby-talk. If married couples from the regular worshipping congregation are invited and come, such a service provides an occasion when the fellowship of the Church and that of the small family circles at least touch and may overlap. Pram services for young mothers who want to worship, and who find a midweek afternoon easier than a Sunday, are sometimes arranged. But the priest should make it clear that he is more interested in the good of marriage than in filling the pews. He is concerned with the deepest happiness of those who ask at their wedding for God's blessing on their marriage. When the world begins to see that the Church is concerned with Christian marriage for its own sake, though it may not respond yet the good news will have been preached in action.

8

MINISTRY TO THE SICK
AND DYING

PARISHIONERS with even the slenderest connections with the Church expect the vicar to call when they are ill. Their motives may not always be clear. Two or three generations ago, the vicar would have been the obvious person to whom to turn for much practical help now provided by the welfare state. Perhaps the frustration and sense of need beyond what may be expected of medical service make people look to the priest, though increasingly they reveal these frustrations to the doctor. Anxieties and boredom and bad personal relationships not only cause some illnesses directly but also directly affect the patient's ability to respond to treatment when illness does occur. For whatever reason people expect the vicar to call when they are ill, there is no question that if he does not do so the fact is both noticed and resented. How a priest is expected to know that a parishioner is ill is not always clear, and priests often complain that they are not sent for as a doctor might be in time of illness. There is much misunderstanding here, for the role of the priest is not that of a medical auxiliary; he does not get called in to attend to a part of the patient which the doctor cannot touch. He comes as a man of God, to embody and express God's concern for one of his children in a time of weakness. When he was ordered deacon, he was told to 'search for the sick'. To search means more than waiting to be told, and an effective parochial intelligence service is one way of actively discovering when parishioners are ill. If the parish priest visits all his parishioners often, he is far more likely to be told when they are ill, and his visits at such times will be more welcome and more effective.

The parish priest will naturally try to keep on the friendliest terms with local doctors, but the difference of approach within a similarity of aim should be recognised by each. Each is concerned with the well-being and wholeness of the patient. The doctor's concern for the patient is focused in his attention to the complaint suffered by the patient. This does not mean that the patient and his illness can be separated and the doctor who knows the patient as a person will be better able both to diagnose the nature of the disorder and to treat the complaint. The priest's concern for the disease is focused in his attention to the person who is ill at ease; he comes to express God's love for the patient.

Before the priest sets out to visit, he will pray that he may be most fully used by God in the situation. If his visit is likely to be unexpected, he will pray that God will prepare the patient to welcome the concern which he comes to bring. He will pray that God will guard his lips and direct his manner that he may convey assurance and not fear, love and not criticism, solemn joy and not flippancy. He will pray that, in addition to the scripture which he may carry in his pocket, he may be filled with Christ's love and make it known, and that his visit may be as literally as possible a god-send to the patient. He goes to say four things, whether implicitly or explicitly. The patient is not forgotten by God or by the Church. The patient's sickness is not a private concern between him and his doctor, though details of the illness may well be confidential, but the whole family of God is affected by the fact that one of God's children is ill. (Of course, the priest will not say it like that to the patient, but his presence and manner should convey what lies behind this fact.) Secondly, he will want to express that wholeness is a gift that God wants us to have. This he may do in many ways, from indicating that the doctor is a man who is doing God's work to an assurance that the local church will pray for the patient by name (on Sunday at 9.45 a.m., for instance). In some cases he may feel it right to read from scripture some passage which makes clear God's concern for the sick. Thirdly, the priest will try to help the sick man use his sickness and not just endure it. It can be a time, for instance, when he appreciates more those kindnesses which in the busy life of health he took for granted. Gratitude and love and patience are among the Christlike qualities which can be deepened during a spell of illness. Fourthly, the patient with a chronic illness can help other weak people by his prayers, for they will come from a more understanding context. The priest can tell the patient of some other sick person and ask him to pray (maybe with the aid of a written prayer on a card) each day at a particular time. In this way a fellowship of prayer among the sick can be built up in a parish and beyond.

The priest will remember that joy and health go together. He will speak of good things he has seen or heard locally, for the patient with the aid of radio or television may be in touch with the world at large but visitors provide his touch with the local community. He will pray briefly with him (not just for him) and give him a blessing. Finally he tells him when he will come again, and comes when he says he will. If the patient is likely to be ill for a long period, visits should be planned on a strictly regular basis so that it is known just when the priest will be coming. It might be every Thursday at 11 o'clock, or the first Tuesday of the month at 3.30 p.m., but if the day and the hour is known the housebound person can look forward to it for some time ahead; the priest's visit becomes one of the reliable things in life when many other fixed points are missing.

If the sickness is such that the person concerned is likely to be housebound more or less permanently, the priest will seek to ensure that the home is part of the fellowship of the Church. If the local congregation remembers him by name at certain fixed times, he can pray for them also, for instance, when he hears the church bell. The idea of a prayer circle takes on more meaning. Often a sick person can do small jobs, the greatest value of which is that he is enabled to feel used and useful. A lay person may be asked to take the job to his house (e.g. envelopes to be addressed, etc.), thus providing occasion for contact with the regular congregation. The priest will try to help the sick person use his enforced leisure to grow in prayer. If the patient is a communicant, or takes the opportunity to become one, the priest will stress the meaning of Communion as an extension of the fellowship of the Church rather than as medicine for the soul. Others members of the family can be encouraged to be present. Some priests will make a point of taking to the house bread and wine recently consecrated at a Communion in church, to emphasise the sense of unity with the Church's offering there. Others will prefer to celebrate Holy Communion in the house, if possible with others present. In either case, the sick person is helped to realise his fellowship with Christ in his Body, the Church.

When the patient is taken to hospital, the position of the parish priest is slightly changed as there is probably a chaplain appointed to the hospital. The priest will still visit, but there is a sense in which he is visiting in somebody else's 'parish', and all the courtesies involved will be observed. It is true that normally doors are open, and bells do not have to be rung to gain admittance, but the priest who asks 'May I . . .?' is easily distinguished from those who would presume. His relationship with the patient is slightly different from that of the hospital chaplain, who looks at the hospital as a whole. The parish priest sees the patient as a detached member of his parish. Not only the patient, but very many others in the hospital who cannot help seeing him, will judge the Master he serves and the Church he represents by the dress and speech and manner of the visiting priest.

The priest will do what he can to prompt occasions of thanksgiving in the patient's mind, for it happens often that the patient rebels through a sense of frustration or anxiety. So by asking questions, he will help the patient to realise that many people are working to hasten his recovery, that his family show their love and care by coming to visit, that the nurses are cheerful and kind and so on. He may ask if he has seen the hospital chaplain, whose responsibility it would be to minister Communion in the hospital. He will pray a prayer of thanksgiving for the good things the patient has mentioned and give him a blessing. If possible, he will avoid those visiting hours when relations and friends come in. If the hospital is distant, a telephone call in advance can avoid many wasted journeys; it is most frustrating after a long drive to discover that the patient has just been taken to the theatre for some further examination. On his return home, he makes a note which ensures that the patient is remembered in the prayers of the Church.

Since in broad terms it may be said that we recover from all sicknesses except the last, normal sick visiting looks forward to recovery and to the patient taking some place again in home life and society. There is thus a distinction between ministry to the dying and normal sick visiting, and the priest has a distinctive ministry to exercise to the dying and to their relatives. His task is made more difficult for him if he waits till death is imminent before he begins to exercise this ministry. While some people have pleurisy, or appendicitis, or a broken leg, all people are going to die. The central symbol of the Christian faith relates to death, and our gospel is good news of eternal life. The worldly conspiracy not to talk about death, especially with those about to experience it, is not a Christian attitude. The priest will preach about death and its meaning; he will find the youth club very ready to discuss the subject. If he teaches that each day can be seen as life in miniature, he can help the people to pray 'Grant us a quiet night and a perfect end'.

In a parish of 10,000 souls there will be, on average, three deaths each week, though they will not be evenly distributed through the year. This does mean, however, that a parish priest in the course of his life's work will have occasion to minister to the dying several thousand times. If he knows himself to be the servant of the risen Christ, this becomes a joyful opportunity. Knowing that perfect love casts out fear, and that God is love, he will seek to bring the dying man into such awareness of God that his fears are banished. These fears are likely to be of four kinds. There is the fear of dying itself, lest it be painful. In fact the medical profession does all in its power to remove the ground of this fear. When we do have pain, we are glad if we can sleep; for patients with a painful terminal illness, death can be a relief to be welcomed were it not for other fears. There is the fear of loneliness. One by one, the associations of this life have to be abandoned; finally even the most intimate of friends and family must be left behind. This is precisely where the priest has good news, for Christ may be known and is present on both sides of death. Life in him which we can share now is not affected by physical death; death has no more dominion over him (Romans 6.9). The opportunity to bring a man to an awareness of this truth is a privilege, and the response of those who come to that awareness is an abiding reward. There is in some the fear of punishment, and the priest has a particular ministry to those whose conscience is burdened with sin and a responsibility to exercise that ministry. This is explicitly stated in the rubrics of the Visitation of the Sick in the Book of Common Prayer. There is also a general fear of the unknown, and that sense of mystery which belongs to anything which we can do once only and from which there is no turning back. Here the priest is able to point to Christ who alone can throw light on what is otherwise unknown; he will speak of what the scripture says about the life to come, of its joy and fellowship, of its freedom from pain and sorrow and parting.

In spite of the attempts made to keep from the dying the truth about their situation, the patient is often aware of the fact. If he trusts the priest, he may share his awareness with him. It is not for the priest to pretend to be a doctor, or to make the doctor's work more difficult by criticism behind his back. If challenged outright, he can honestly reply 'I am not a medical man and I do not know; but if, in fact, you did only have a few weeks left what are the most important things you would do?' Alternatively after disclaiming medical knowledge, he could ask 'Apart from the sorrow it would give your family, are you yourself ready for it?' There are times when the dying man and his family are trying to bluff one another, and the priest is charged by each side not to tell the other. This is an unhappy situation, and if love is stronger than death it were better and happier that a married couple face the situation together. If they are together now in Christ, and can grasp that neither life nor death nor any created thing can separate them from God's love in Christ, then they will still be together in Christ even when the death of one separates them on earth. The comfort to a man once he knows that his wife also knows, and knows also that she will be with him when the time comes, is something very real. If husband and wife can share in Communion in the home together and the emphasis of the priest's teaching is on Christ's promise that 'I am with you always', the couple can be brought closer together and their love deepened. While the priest will not exaggerate the penitential element, lest the patient should feel that his sickness is the reward for his sin, he can point out that sin is going one's own way and that now Christ is saying 'Come to me'. If confession is seen as an acknowledgment with penitence of having gone one's own way, then absolution is seen as an assurance by God that one is not rejected. If, instead of living for ourselves and so dying by ourselves, we live for Christ, though bodily we may die our life is hid with Christ in God. The element of offering in the Communion takes on a new meaning for as the life which was offered for us is offered to us, so in dying we can offer our body and its life to him. The priest will encourage the sick man to reflect on his blessings and to believe that 'so long thy power hath led me, sure it still will lead me on'.

When the time to die comes close, the priest may be asked to anoint the patient. This ministry should by no means be confined to the dying and many priests who use it can tell of patients so strengthened that their recovery from illness took on new vigour after they were anointed. For the dying it is a preparation for a holy death. If the family can be there and the anointing can be done in the context of Holy Communion, its meaning is most clearly seen. There is no form provided in the Book of Common Prayer, though the Convocation of Canterbury in 1935, and that of York in 1936, approved orders for Administration of Holy Unction and the Laying-on of hands.[1] A similar and simpler order is contained in Bishop L. S. Hunter's *Diocesan Service Book*,[2] and there is a simple form published by the Guild of St Raphael.[3]

Priests differ in their opinions concerning whether anointing and laying-on of hands should be ministered once and for all, or whether they should be repeated. The argument against repetition is that it seems to introduce an element of doubt as to the effectiveness of the previous occasion. If the patient has made a particular act of aligning his will with that of God, with penitence and faith, it would seem right to minister anointing once. Before a major operation this would clearly be so. The ministry of Holy Communion would seem the right occasion for the patient to give thanks for blessings received, and to renew his penitence and act of faith. Some priests lay their hands on the head of the patient when giving the blessing at such a Communion, but this is not the formal laying-on of hands.

The priest will have to be guided by the situation itself in deciding whether to stay or leave when the onset of death is imminent. My personal experience is that I have usually regretted the occasions when I have left. Just to be there, as an outward and visible reminder to the dying man and his family that they are not alone, is a priestly act. As faculties fail and memory recedes, anything that is said must be of the simplest. Even when all form of recognition seems to have gone, phrases such as 'Jesus says: I am with you' or the Lord's Prayer spoken clearly may evoke a response. It is said that usually hearing is the last faculty to be lost and it is good that the name of Jesus should be the last sound heard in this life by those who look to him as the source of eternal life.

If the priest is present when death comes, he will pray at once with the family commending the passing soul to God. He will

[1] Acts of the Convocations of Canterbury and York. SPCK, 1971, pp. 72–86.
[2] Oxford University Press, 1965, pp. 103–10.
[3] Guild of St Raphael, 77 Kinnerton Street, London, S.W.1.

then leave unless specifically asked to stay. If he has come to be trusted by the family he may be asked for guidance on such matters as whether the children should see the body or how they should tell a five-year-old. There are no universal rules, but there are some guide-lines. Only the truth should be told and that in language that can be understood, If a child is told that his father has gone to be with Jesus, it may be necessary to explain why the body is still in the bedroom. Again, it is Daddy's old body and not Daddy himself who is buried. In general, it is probably better to allow children to see the now disused body than to be excluded from what older relations and friends are allowed to share. Again, unless the surviving parent is hysterical, it is better that children should be told intimate family news by a parent and not by the priest. The parish priest is likely to be asked for advice and information about registering the death, about undertakers and funeral arrangements. Guidance in these practical matters is a real ministry. During the few days between the death and the funeral there will be much for the family to do, and many people at hand to help. A brief call by the priest during this period to agree any plans for the service and to inquire whether any help is needed is as much first-hand contact as is likely to be needed. Unknown to the family, however, he may ask church members who live near by to be ready to offer mundane help (such as taking care of the dog on the day of the funeral, or doing some shopping to avoid embarrassment from the inquisitive) which they are prepared either to be accepted or declined. The priest will have ample contacts with the family after the funeral when he can minister to them as they adjust to grief.

9
FUNERALS AND THE BEREAVED

Too often, even with the help of a parochial intelligence service, the first intimation the priest receives of a death in the parish is a call from the undertaker who has been in touch with the family and fixed up almost all the arrangements for the funeral service. The wise priest will take trouble to cultivate good relations with the local undertakers; they are likely to have to co-operate for some years to help families whose nerves are on edge. When the priest hears from the undertaker about a death in the parish, he will call at the house at the first opportunity, having discovered whether the body has been removed to a chapel of rest. He will also check that the timing of his visit does not coincide with the moment when the body is to be placed in the coffin. The priest's visit to the house will be prompt and brief, but not hasty. The number of things that need to be done and the probable state of shock which affects the family preclude any protracted visiting. After the few moments needed to assess the reactions of the family, the priest will agree the details of any funeral arrangements, taking full responsibility for the service itself, and will invite the family to pray before he leaves. If asked to see the body, it is, in my opinion, right to do so and to pray at that point of the visit.

The funeral service itself is likely to be an ordeal which is feared by the immediate family and an occasion for showing respect to the deceased and sympathy to the family by others who are present. It can easily be a very impersonal occasion, with a large element of superstition and wishful thinking. Yet it is significant that though many children are not baptised in infancy

77

and very many marriages take place with no religious service, a funeral without a religious ceremony is very rare indeed. The evangelistic opportunity of a funeral can easily be exaggerated, but it is a meeting-point of priest and people and the harm done by a funeral conducted without sensitivity and conviction can be great.

The wise priest will have learned the funeral service by heart so that he may be master of the situation and not the servant of the book. With all the distraction that comes with entering the church in procession and moving to the chancel step and the placing of the coffin on the stools, the priest may reserve some of the opening sentences until the mourners are in their places. Copies of the service, which should be all alike, should be provided for everybody present if there is to be any participation, and the priest will give detailed instructions so that the people can follow. If the order of the service has a choice of readings, he will tell the people which one he is using; a word of explanation before the reading and even before each prayer is helpful. If there are hymns,· the priest will have discussed with the family which hymns they want and why. They must be well known since there will be those present who are not church-goers, but it is not necessary to be tied down to Crimond and 'Abide with me'; the latter is more appropriate before death than at a funeral. Hymns that speak of resurrection and Christian hope and the love of God can be commended, such as the Easter hymn 'Jesus lives' or 'Thine for ever, God of love'. Though the connection is not obvious at first, the hymn 'As with gladness men of old' makes a very suitable hymn for a funeral.

The Order of Service for the Burial of the Dead[1] makes no provision for a sermon nor are the mourners ready to sit back and listen to a long dissertation. But a message of Christian hope and confidence, an assurance that death cannot separate us from the love of God in Christ, and a pointing forwards rather than back

---

[1] The ASB has a rubric, 'A sermon may be preached'.

to that life which has just ended, can be a word from God to those in sorrow. A Christian funeral is not an occasion for an eulogy of the deceased, for the hope of the Christian does not rest in his good deeds or qualities but in the death and resurrection of Jesus and in the love, mercy and power of God. The very brief sermon may be given conveniently after the lesson and before the prayers; alternatively a short explanation of the meaning of the lesson may be used to express the Christian hope.

The committal should be reverent and brief. It is convenient if the coffin can be lowered before the sentences or the verses from the psalm are said, as little attention is paid until this happens. Customs vary in regard to casting earth and in some places all the immediate family share in this; this is much to be preferred to the practice of giving the priest a small phial of silver sand, a refinement which takes away the simple meaning of 'earth to earth'. If the priest is not a complete stranger to the deceased and his family, the practice of using the Christian name at the committal has meaning and is appreciated. This is provided for in the ASB Order of Service. The words which were heard as a voice from heaven can be said with a loud voice, and the ascription to God at the close likewise.

Naturally the family mourners will want to see the grave where the coffin lies, but that is looking back instead of forward. The priest will wait till they have done this, will greet the immediate family and tell them when he will next call to see them, and will then discreetly depart to disrobe and pray, and then move on to his next task. Unless he knows the family well, or unless offence would be given, there is little value in being present at the funeral tea.

When there is a cremation, the procedure is almost exactly similar if the first part of the service is taken in church and the committal only at the crematorium. However, there will be just a few people who may not have come to the church who do come to the committal, so that the introduction of some opening sentences and the Lord's Prayer before the committal makes the service a little less stark in its brevity. On the other hand, the whole service may take place in the crematorium chapel and the committal may precede the readings and psalm and prayers if the priest so wishes. If the priest varies the normal order he must arrange with the official on duty in advance and discover what method is used to indicate that he has reached this point in the service. If the priest is taking either a funeral or a cremation because he is doing duty on some rota system, it is time and money well spent to send a card to the incumbent of the parish where the deceased lived; it is possible he may not know of the death. There are, of course, plenty of difficulties in a large city in discovering the parish concerned but these are not insuperable.

When the funeral is over, the priest has a ministry to the family which can be of great value. For reasons which are partly social and partly psychological, there seem to be certain times when this ministry is most valued. About a week after the funeral, letters having been written and the flowers faded, friends and relations having expressed their sympathy, the immediate family begin to realise what has happened. Again after anything from one to three months, there is liable to be a period of rebellion against the facts when the hope of salvation by activity is wearing thin. The anniversary of the death understandably brings it all back but also seems to be a period of depression. The priest will notice three common alternatives to Christian hope to which he can minister. There is an acceptance of the fact of bereavement, with a determination to grin and bear it. Tears are despised. The fact cannot be altered so life must be resumed with energy. A more extreme symptom of this is when reminders of the deceased, photographs and familiar objects, are put away and even disposed of. This reaction to grief is stoic rather than Christian. It tends to deny sorrow and so to deny love and its embodiment. The priest can help by encouraging conversation about the deceased; he can point out that there is no shame in tears and grief and, indeed, that they are (normally) evidence of love. A card or letter on the anniversary of the death is important when the family adopt this attitude. The dangers of unwise, or even foolhardy, activity are there and there is the possibility of a breakdown.

A second reaction to grief, at the other end of the scale, is self-pity when the bereaved wife feels her loss is greater than anybody else's. It is true that no third party knows just how they loved one another, but the dangers which can follow in the wake of self-pity are great. It is important that such people avoid solitariness. They are likely to counter any direct efforts by the priest to become involved in any social activity, and may refuse to come to church because it brings it all back. It is possible sometimes to persuade others to ask them to do small tasks, as a favour, which enable them to meet people; small children are the most likely to work their way into such hearts.

A third and common reaction to grief is despair, which may turn to anger and bitterness. There is a mixture of 'what have I done to deserve this?' with a consequent transfer of the blame to some other person or body, and 'how can I live without him?' The earthly answers that the world is not against them, that doctors and nurses did all they could, that other people do care, are commonly rejected. The ultimate answer is that the Cross and Resurrection of Jesus show that God does care and that there is a future. The priest must, by faithful visiting, show that he cares because God cares. There is the possibility that despair may lead to illness which will need medical or psychiatric care; there is the alternative possibility that in reaction the bereaved person will snatch at some way out of despair, maybe a second marriage (which may prove to be very happy), or may turn to alcohol to drown sorrow (which may prove to be very unhappy for him and others).

Whatever the reaction, grief is a shock, the pain of which is not felt till after a period of numbness. The priest will learn all he can from others about the characteristics of grief and will minister with tenderness and wisdom to those members of God's family for which he has a special responsibility who have to suffer grief. He will find many allies, among them the Cruse Clubs, which help widows in many practical problems relating to grants, children's education, holidays and similar matters which can be the cause of anxiety to a widow. The priest will find it valuable to keep the Sunday after All Saints Day for remembering by name those who have died in the past year. A letter sent to each family to which this applies gives them the opportunity to share in this act. Some will not come, but the value of the act must not be measured by the extent of the response. In all he does, the priest is not using grief as an occasion to recruit new worshippers, but is acting as the servant of Christ who is the resurrection and the life.

10
PARISH ADMINISTRATION

It is impossible to generalise about the work of administration of parishes when they vary from under a hundred souls in the heart of the country to twenty thousand or more souls in an industrial city. Yet in any parish the incumbent will be involved in some committee work and some ministry of correspondence in his study. There will be at the least a Parochial Church Council, of which he will be chairman, and an Annual Parochial Church Meeting and a Deanery Synod; there will be some forms to complete and returns to make, even if they are only nil returns of marriages made to the Superintendent Registrar of Births, Marriages and Deaths.

The parish priest will naturally make himself familiar with the law in regard to churchwardens, the power to appoint or dismiss an organist, the rights of parishioners in regard to burial and memorials in the churchyard and kindred matters. However, there is more to running a happy parish than seeing that the rights of each person are safeguarded. The parish priest is the leader of a team whose task is to set forward the Kingship of Christ in the parish, and the maintenance of the team and guidance of its work is the particular responsibility of the priest. First and foremost, he will establish good relations with the churchwardens, sharing his views with them and hearing their views from them. It is true that many of the powers of churchwardens are now exercised jointly with the Parochial Church Council, but the churchwardens are to a large extent the spokesmen of the Council. Time spent in discussing parochial policy with the churchwardens is time well spent. If there is a small Standing Committee (perhaps of the vicar and wardens, the treasurer and secretary of the PCC), an evening spent discussing the matters to be considered at the next

Council meeting will be amply repaid. The fact that the Church Council controls the spending of money given through the collections may be a rather earthly factor but is one important reason for maintaining good relations! If the Sunday School needs to be equipped adequately, or new hymn-books are needed, or a new mower required for the churchyard, the incumbent cannot act on his own unless he is prepared to pay the bill. Quite apart from these mundane reasons, the Parochial Church Council and the incumbent form the executive committee for undertaking the work of the parish. That work is not limited to the maintenance of the plant, though it includes it. The worship of God, declaring his praise and proclaiming the good news, is the first priority. The priest is the ordained leader of the corporate worship of the local church, but it is the worship of the body which he leads. The Parochial Church Council can and should discuss the way the parish worships, and the times at which services are held; it should discuss also how the young are to be brought up in the faith, and what steps should be taken to proclaim the gospel to those who appear to ignore it.

If the parish is large, the PCC may appoint a variety of sub-committees to pay special attention to the work of youth clubs, stewardship, Sunday schools, overseas missionary work, social responsibility, publicity and other such matters. While the incumbent may have a right to sit on all such sub-committees, it does not follow that he should attend all their meetings. From time to time, a meeting of the chairmen or secretaries of all such small committees will help to co-ordinate their activities and thinking. Attendance by the priest (as by the lay representatives) at the deanery synod is necessary if the parish is to take its proper place in the life of the Church as a whole.

Apart from such meetings which belong to the organised structure of the Church, the priest will need to spend time with the leaders of each organisation in the parish. If he does not, the organisations may easily pursue a course of their own, independent of the life and purpose of the parish. Thus an hour spent each month with the organist and choirmaster discussing not only the music for the coming month, but also the pastoral care of the choirboys and other choristers, is a way in which working together can be promoted. The choirmaster ought to be told if a chorister is preparing for confirmation, or has a sick father; equally the priest should be told of irregular attendance by a boy, for it may be a symptom of some difficulty at home over which he can help. Similar meetings with leaders of youth organisations, Sunday school teachers and others are part of the priest's involvement in the smooth running of a parish.

The particular task of the priest in all such meetings is, as in other forms of leadership, to do three things. In the first place to see that the activity of each group or organisation serves the ulti-mate purpose of the Church in the parish, which is to acknow-ledge and to declare the sovereignty of God in Christ. Some groups may appear to serve that purpose only indirectly; other groups may have to be encouraged to look at their own aims and structure so that they may see whether they serve the ultimate purposes of God at all. When resources of time and money and leaders are limited, the priest is responsible for guiding the parish to use its resources in the wisest way.

In the second place the priest exercises his leadership by keeping the various organisations and their leaders working together as a team, each recognising that the others are directed to the same ultimate end. The principal way in which this may be shown is by the common offering of all such parochial activity at the Parish Eucharist. The leaders and officers of parish organisations should be given occasion to know one another. In a small country parish there is no problem; in a big city or suburban parish, this can be a very real problem. In addition, when one organisation is planning its programme or reshaping its policy, it is for the priest to see that the policy or programme does not clash in any serious way with that of another organisation.

In the third place, the parish priest is always on the watch for new leaders. This is especially true in suburban parishes with a high mobility rate, though the effect on parish life of modern mobility is sometimes over-rated. The families most likely to be on the move probably do so because the principal breadwinner has a chance of promotion or a better job, but this kind of person is also usually willing to accept some degree of responsibility in a parish. The priest cannot possibly find the right leaders unless he knows the people well, which includes knowing them at home; a man's attitude to his own children will help the priest to decide whether he would make a suitable superintendent for the Sunday school. Without visiting, it is hard to see how the priest can pick leaders for the parochial team or know whether the tasks he has asked them to do are adversely affecting their home life.

One side of parochial administration, then, is related to team-work and the time involved is spent largely in meeting and causing others to meet. The other side broadly comprises office work, but it not to be despised for being so called. In any occupation there are letters to be written, records to be kept and notes to make for future reference. The amount of time which this involves, even in a large town parish, is often exaggerated. Some of this may be impersonal and the incumbent may have to deal with local contractors about repairs to the church roof or levelling the graveyard. Most of this work has a personal and often emotional element, however. The wording of an inscription on a tombstone is a matter of real significance. Should the priest attempt to challenge the words 'Thy will be done' on the grave-stone of a child killed in a motor accident, or 'Asleep in Jesus' on that of a man who drank himself to death? Simple letters, asking if one can attend a meeting on Friday week, can be simply answered; others call for prayer and for a reply with a genuine personal touch. If the priest can type reasonably, it makes it much easier to keep copies of letters referring to future engagements. Some circular letters, duplicated and signed, may be sent out. The kind of parish where the priest cannot find a volunteer to help do this work tidily is also likely to be the kind of parish where the need for circular letters is small.

Correspondence is a ministry, and much form-filling can be a ministry. The application form for reading banns of marriage is charged with personal concern and should only be handled with prayer for those whose names are on it. Priests vary in their attitude to card-index systems. The purpose of any such system is to save time by being methodical, and to save strain on one's memory. Some things are easily remembered and few vicars would need to look up the telephone number of their church-wardens each time they made a call, but they would not despise the telephone directory which is a simple filing system. To save one's memory, lists of visiting preachers, annual accounts, dates of committee meetings in the past year, orders of service for special occasions and similar matters can be filed in some methodical order. The local civil electoral register, which can be purchased, provides as valuable a visiting list as one can find. Dates of visits and any other simple facts can easily be inserted in the margin, and these marginal marks quickly give an indication if the priest's visiting is geographically one-sided. For church members, the priest may care to have cards with names and dates of birth of children and any other matter which will provide material for his prayers. A book kept either in the study or on his prayer desk, containing the names and addresses of couples he has married and families where a member has died, can also help him in his prayers. Records are not kept for their own sake but that the priest may do his work better and more easily. If part of that work is to make known God's concern for his children, then there is a real difference between asking how Mary and James are and having to ask whether there are any children in the family. If a young couple, having been married on the seventeenth day of a month, know that the priest who married them will remember them by name on the seventeenth day of every month in his prayers, at least they know that somebody cares; some will realise that God cares. One danger to be avoided is to become so card-index conscious that persons become names on a card. The other dangers of time wasted through inefficiency and apparent lack of concern through avoidable forgetfulness are probably greater.

The ministry of correspondence is an extension of the ministry of visiting. Through the medium of the letter, there is a meeting of two people. The meeting is at second hand and for that very reason there is all the more need for sensitivity, since one cannot compensate for misunderstanding by any change in tone of voice or smile or other gesture. It is one thing to state a point or a question in a letter, to reply to a question or to comment on an opinion. It is another thing for the comment or question to be understood in the way intended. If prayer for another means to let the operation be taken up into the activity of God, then letter writing becomes part of prayer and vice versa. This is not a separation of two activities, praying first and then writing the letter. It is rather that deliberate effort to enter into the feeling of him to whom the letter is written, to sense anxiety and hope or even guilty fear and to write so that God's caring love may be more likely to work in the heart of the recipient.

Of course this point can be exaggerated. Accepting or declining an invitation to speak to some group in a neighbouring parish is not in the same class as a letter of condolence or of advice in some difficult domestic problem; yet written with love and prayer, all such letters become part of a ministry of caring. Perhaps sensitivity to the deep feelings of others and the desire that needs be met is of the essence of intercessory prayer. It certainly turns letter writing into a joy rather than a chore. In theory the same applies to the telephone; the sudden intrusion of the double ringing tone makes prayerful sensitivity less easy, but the principles are exactly the same.

A further administrative task is the production of the parish magazine, an opportunity for communication which most organisations would envy. The magazine is likely to go into the homes of many who do not come to church but have a measure of goodwill and, because it is paid for in most cases, each copy is likely to be read by more than one person. The incumbent is able to write something which will be read by those who are not present to hear him preach. The message, or Vicar's Letter, needs as much care as a sermon, and Christian comment on matters of local concern will be read; comments on matters of international concern are less likely to be read. It is noticeable how readers of really local newspapers turn to reports of events which they have attended to see if the reporter reacted as they did, and whether the name of a friend or their own name appears in the list of prizewinners. In the same way, local church news with a record of the involvement of individuals is important matter for the magazine. Articles on practical Christian living in the local context, and news about churches of other denominations in the neighbourhood and of deanery and diocesan activities, are worth inserting. The writing of the parish magazine becomes a burden when it is left till the last minute, and the Vicar's Letter has to be written and other matter assembled in time to catch the post. In a small parish, the task of distributing and even duplicating the magazine may fall on the vicar. In this, as in many other things, the vicar of a large town parish is likely to be able to call on sufficient help to reduce his share to that of producing the written matter on time.

In a very large parish, and in some city churches where a ministry is exercised to the city as well as to a geographical parish, some secretarial help may be needed. The danger of weakening the personal link between priest and people must be watched. The parish priest is not running a business; his task is a mixture of leading a team and shepherding a flock. The extent of the administrative work and the way in which it is regarded as a necessary evil depends on the attitude of the priest to his work. This question has been examined in some detail by Dr P. F. Rudge.[1] In general, the time spent on paper-work which is necessary for the smooth running of the parish need not be great, and most of it is personal contact at second hand and occasion for prayer, each of which is an essential part of the life of a priest.

[1] P. F. Rudge, *Ministry and Management* (Tavistock Publications, 1968).

In all this, one great danger to be avoided is that of being, or even seeming to be, so busy that people are hesitant to come to the vicar. It cannot be emphasised too strongly that the parish priest is not ordained to run a business. He must have time, and be known to have time, for people and for prayer. He must have time for his family which may call for quite a measure of self-discipline, as his busiest hours are likely to be those when his children are at home in the evenings. This self-discipline means that he must be the master and not the slave of his diary. The words 'Day Off' should be firmly written in ink, and only the most urgent calls on his personal attention allowed to interfere. This is part of his duty to himself, let alone to his wife and family. (The cheerfulness and faithfulness of so many clergy wives whose husbands make little leisure time to share with them is beyond praise.) The priest himself needs leisure to re-create himself, and those who boast of having had so few Sundays away in the last so many years should rather apologise. Perhaps rural deans, and even bishops, should do more to encourage the clergy, for whom they have a responsibility, to have adequate holidays and should actively plan for Readers and retired clergy to cover the Sunday services.

There are limits to the size of a vicarage garden, and one garden fête in the summer is not a sufficient justification for a garden which requires several hours of lawn-mowing each week. On the other hand, a little hard digging gets a lot of frustrations out of the system besides making possible a supply of fresh vegetables. If not gardening, some leisure activity or the pursuit of a hobby is good for both soul and body; there is nothing unspiritual about being in the village cricket team (or playing for England, if you are good enough), singing in the local choral society, collecting wild flowers or whatever one's interest happens to be. The parish priest is often called the parson; it is important that he should be a person, and not the head of an administrative machine.

11

TEAMWORK IN A PARISH

THE Measure[1] which defined the duty of the Parochial Church Council 'to co-operate with the incumbent in the initiation, conduct and development of Church work both within the parish and outside' was, in its time, a step forward in the relation of laity and clergy in the Church. Yet Institution Services for a long time invited the people not only to pray for their vicar but to 'help him forward in his holy calling'. The image of the Church as an organisation, divided into parishes for efficient working, with the church building as its centre and the priest as its local agent, is the simple image which very closely reflected the position of the Church of England. Against this loud voices of protest have been raised. The Church, it is rightly pointed out, is the people not just the priests. Mission, service and intercession are part of the priestly work which belongs to the body as a whole. The task of the ordained priest is seen as ministering to the laity in such a way that they can do their proper work in the world.

It may be that sociological factors have contributed very largely to theological rethinking about the structure and role of the Church in society. Similar factors, in particular that of hunger, made the prodigal son rethink his role in the family home. A shortage of clergy, coupled with the move of people from country to city,[2] has hastened the process of thinking. Clearly the problem is not how lay people can best help the clergy, but how clergy and laity should properly work together in the common task of the

---

[1] Parochial Church Councils (Powers) Measure 1921, Section 2.
[2] This move is gradually going in reverse. Cities in England are growing smaller; commuter suburbs and villages are growing. See *Census 1971, England and Wales. Preliminary Report* (HMSO, 1971).

Church. In many dioceses, the Service of Institution of new incumbents has been wholly rewritten to emphasise the relationship which should exist between fellow-workers.

A village or small country town, where the parish priest knew every family well and where the parish registers contained the history of the village, was for so long the norm of English parochial life that the image dies a slow death. There are still thousands of such parishes, though the process of pairing and grouping is accelerating. However clearly bishops and priests may see this as a means of godly co-operation, churchwardens (at least at first) see it as a necessary evil due to the shortage of money and manpower. The danger is that so long as money and men can be found to staff very small parishes, the people are liable to leave everything to the priest and so will not grow in this particular aspect of Christian living.

In a city or large suburban parish it is obvious that the parish priest cannot know everybody well nor do the visiting, interviewing and occasional offices single-handed. Thus in the parish where I served as a Reader in 1935, there were (in addition to the vicar) six curates, one retired priest who helped occasionally, two whole-time lay workers, two voluntary Readers and a parish nurse. Times have changed. There used to be district visitors, lay people who shared in visiting the sick and lonely, but they did not live in the districts they visited.

Various factors have led to the development of an Area Leader system in many large parishes. Street wardens in the days of war acting as local air raid wardens, and local leaders appointed as a result of stewardship campaigns, helped to establish the pattern. An 'area' of a parish is little more or less than a parish in miniature, a thousand people being a manageable size. The parish priest chooses a married couple living in the area as the representatives of the church in that area. Thus in a parish of 12,000 souls a dozen couples form a pastoral team under the leadership of the vicar. The purpose of the scheme and the many ways in which it can develop can be explained and explored as the team meets with the priest, and the vision of the team as representatives of the Church doing its work and not just helping the priest do his can grow clearer. Thus the team does not exist just to keep the vicar informed about domestic crises, so that he can visit. When the vicar discovers any such crisis, he will inform the area leaders so that they can visit. Each Area Leader will soon realise that more local help is needed, and a team of half a dozen couples in an area may prove to be a convenient size. The task of the local group is no less than the task of the Church, that is to say service, intercession and mission in ascending order of difficulty. Local visitors, living in the road or street or block of flats for which they have responsibility, will know of sickness and of good fortune of the people in their road; they will know when residents leave or newcomers arrive. Understandably they will inform the vicar through the Area Leader, but they will not leave it to him alone to act. Either on their own initiative, or after consultation with the Area Leader and the local group, they will take local action themselves. If, for example, a boy or girl in the area is being prepared for confirmation the priest will tell the Area Leader who can keep in touch, or make contact with the family and see that others of a similar age know and encourage the candidate. Similar information about newly married couples, bereavements, coming and going of residents, enable priest and people alike to exercise a ministry of caring for Christ's sake.

This cannot be achieved overnight, and small, easy tasks will be undertaken to give confidence to the workers and cohesion to the team. Thus a parochial project where the task is easily defined may be given to all the local groups as an exercise. Such a task might be the wider distribution of the parish magazine. The team can first learn together why it is thought good to increase circulation, and what purposes the magazine does and can serve. The priest, in return, is likely to discover how parishioners react to the magazine as it is and so make it what it should be. The team could then plan the simple operation of visiting needed to achieve their objective, and in the process of carrying it out vast quantities of information will be gleaned and a great deal learned in respect of local opinion about the Church. Relevant local information will be kept by the Area Leader and used sensibly; for instance, the Baptist minister or Roman priest can be told of sick persons of their persuasion if it is evident that they do not know. Thus an operation with a very simple short-term objective can contribute to ecumenical goodwill, and can open up avenues of neighbourly service which were not at first envisaged. At a later date a more ambitious objective can be set. It might, for instance, be to see that there should be no lonely house-bound person in the parish who shall not in future be without a regular friendly visit. This, of course, would not be confined to Anglicans. Gradually the local teams will develop their own ways of serving their area, and interchange of ideas and projects will take place when the Area Leaders meet together with the priest.

Periodically the priest will visit the home of each Area Leader to meet with the local team for prayer, encouragement, exchange of information and planning. The meeting takes on a richer significance if Communion is celebrated in the home. Some explanation about sitting or standing or kneeling should be given when this is first done, to put the team members at their ease. Some parts of the service, reading the epistle and gospel for example, can be shared and the Area Leader should supply material for the intercession if he does not actually lead it. If the priest brings the vessels and the wine, but the hostess provides a loaf of bread from which a slice is cut, and if coffee is served at the same table after the Communion, the word 'service' seems to take on a new meaning. As a matter of experience, I have found communicants on Sundays increase rather than decrease as a result of such house communion services. There are many practical matters to decide in a house communion as, for instance, whether the priest moves round to minister or whether the bread and the cup is passed round, each person ministering to his neighbour; these matters must, of course, be determined in advance.

After the Communion and subsequent coffee, members of the

group can report on their activities and discuss how best they can serve the area. It is important to see that the Church is not an extra voluntary agency for social work. Just as it is rightly insisted that God is not the God of the gaps in human understanding, so the Church is not an agency to fill in the gaps of the statutory services. Where service is not being offered as it might be, the Church may supply the need; but it will seek to enter and strengthen the existing services and (as in education) do some of its work as a recognised partner of the state. In some fields, the Church can initiate a form of service inviting other people of goodwill to share in it. Where need is to be met, service done is more important than credit won. The Area Leader and the visitors will have detailed knowledge of individuals whose immediate needs (transport to hospital, etc.) can be met by themselves. By all that they do they make that part of the parish a more friendly place in which to live and they themselves become more considerate people. They are helping to build up community in what can otherwise be mere proximity, to bring neighbourliness into neighbourhood. In the whole process, as they pray and read the bible and share hospitality and plan service to the area together with the priest, they become what they are—the Church in the area. The body of Christ is built up as its cells come to life.

The local group under the Area Leader has a larger task than social service in the name of Christ and even intercession. The Church is called not only to serve but to witness. It may be true that what we are speaks louder than what we say, but mission includes both being and saying. The commission of Christ to his Church to teach and preach, and the understanding by the early Church of the role of witness, is clear. The concern of the Church is that the sovereignty of Christ shall be acknowledged in the hearts of men and in the structures of society. This is in contrast with the commonly accepted priorities of affluence, security, status and leisure concerning which the teaching of Jesus has much to say. To preach the good news of Jesus Christ in the context of an apathetic society is not easy. The majority will seldom be in a church and, in an age when the voices of persuasion are heard on all sides, people build up their defences. Yet there are means which the priest and the team in an area of the parish can attempt. Personal invitations to Guest Services do have a response, new-comers do respond to invitations to meet neighbours at coffee mornings and some will respond to an invitation to form a discussion group especially on a short-term basis. One of the most valuable exercises in regard to mission by priest and people in a parish is for each local team to consider how each member came to find faith in Christ and accepted the priorities of the gospel rather than those of contemporary society. If the Holy Spirit has worked in them in this way, then he may equally work in the lives of others in the same way. The local team can then discuss how it can plan its activities so as to co-operate with God the Holy Spirit in drawing men to Christ.

House-groups can be a means of mission and of growth in the body of Christ if guided wisely. They can equally become talking groups with a life of their own divorced from the life of the Church. The principles on which they can work and some of the requirements of the leader are set out in Michael Skinner's book *House Groups*.[1] They are easier to form on a neighbourhood basis if the topic for study is clearly defined and the number of meetings is limited and known in advance. The size of a study-group is a matter to be watched; for short-term work a group should be not less than six nor more than ten people. If the group is too small, there is not sufficient interchange of opinion to justify its existence; if it exceeds ten or twelve persons, the danger of sub-groups forming increases and also individuals feel that they can drop out without affecting the life of the group.

The priest who seeks to use house-groups as a means of evangelism does well to undergo some training himself in their working. There are several courses available where such training is given. Quickly the priest will learn that a group in which there is a dominant figure, expert in the material or subject under discussion

[1] *House Groups*. M. Skinner (Epworth Press and SPCK, 1969).

behaves entirely differently from a group without such a figure. This is not to say that one is better than the other, but the process of learning is quite different. Without such a figure, the more timid member will express his doubts and his convictions in a way otherwise almost impossible; by so doing he becomes an active rather than a passive member of the group. On the other hand, there must be some person in the group whose responsibility it is to see that the group holds together and that members do not drop out either mentally or physically. In due course the whole group accepts this responsibility, if the numbers are not too great.

A house-group can be encouraged to do things together which the members might not do separately; bible-study is one such activity. Members can be led to pray for particular people and causes, to thank God for the good fortune of others and generally to enlarge the area of concern of their prayers. There are groups which consist wholly of church-going members, who meet to do with a few others what cannot be done in the congregation. In such a group, the presence of the priest may be a help and the group meeting provides opportunity to extend his teaching office and pastoral care and to build up the Body of Christ. There can also be groups formed on an area basis with only a few church members, the others being interested but uncommitted, and in such groups the priest's work is better done at second hand. The members already share in common the fact that they are neighbours, but differ in their varying attachment to any church. Instead of facing one another and discussing their differences, in a house-group they face some topic or problem and grow together.

In such a small group, a common language is readily used, whereas the language of the pulpit is sometimes quite different from that of the pew. Friendships can be formed and so links between the church and the neighbours established. This is important, because evangelism can ultimately take place only in fellowship, and the church congregation is likely to be too large and not cohesive enough to provide the kind of fellowship needed. The small group provides acceptance of people as they are, freedom to leave but concern when they do, a welcome when they return and a recognition of honest doubt. To lead such a group without becoming a dominant figure calls for training and the priest, having first had training himself, has the responsibility for equipping leaders for this work. In this he may enlist the help of another priest experienced in Parish Life Conferences and group methods. It is not by techniques that men and women are converted, but by the Holy Spirit, working in the Body of Christ. It is not the priest alone who is called to the work of witness to faith in Christ. By building up a team of lay people who are ready to talk with their neighbours in house-groups, the priest is enabling the Church to do its work of mission in the parish setting.

The building up of a parochial team of this sort does not take away from the parish priest either the duty or the joy of visiting the people of the parish at all times, and not only at times of personal crisis. Naturally when he first arrives in the parish, he will visit the members of the Parochial Church Council, the Sunday school teachers, and all church members who are doing any other work of responsibility in the parish. Naturally he will use the Electoral Roll, Confirmation Registers and other lists of persons who have a recognisable link with the church, and will visit them. He is vicar, however, of the whole parish and as far as he may, he will visit all the parishioners. This has nothing to do with the old adage about a house-going parson making a church-going people, though there is a great deal more truth in the saying than many clergy will admit. Visiting is the best way in which a priest can come to know the people of the parish, and only when he knows them can he properly pray for them; this ministry of intercession is part of his priestly work. There is no question that this kind of visiting is both welcomed and expected. When I go to meetings of Parochial Church Councils in parishes where a new incumbent is to be appointed, practically without exception I am told that what they want is a vicar who will visit everybody.

Perhaps in very large parishes it is not possible to get round to every house; but in any parish the worshipping congregation would be massive indeed if the parish priest was unable to visit anybody else. If the parish priest loves people for Christ's sake, he will find such joy in this visiting that he will want to do it in any case.

12

CONVERSION, CONFESSION AND COUNSEL

THE Church has good news to tell the world. The good news is of the love of God for the world, which he has made known in Jesus Christ. The good news means that the relationship between men and God, broken as a result of human sin, has been restored as a result of the life, death and resurrection of Jesus Christ. When individuals accept this good news for themselves, they are able to turn from self-centred lives to lives centred on God made known in Christ. The precise thought-form in which the good news is presented and the nature of the appeal that is made to persuade people to turn to Christ does differ. The Kingdom of God will not come by re-structuring society but by the conversion of people.

There is a danger in the life of every priest that the pastoral care of individuals, the conduct of services, the care of the church building and the general building up of the life of the parish may be so absorbing that the work of evangelism is smothered. There is no doubt that meeting individuals in connection with baptisms, confirmation, weddings and funerals provides occasions when good news can be declared. But the whole Church, of which the priest is an ordained representative, is called to the task of witness. There are some people, by no means all priests, who are given special, recognisable gifts for evangelism. A few such people, known all over the world, spend their whole time proclaiming the gospel to large crowds of people. These preachers are foremost in pointing out the need for personal care for everyone who responds to their preaching. These preachers are only doing on a large scale in isolated centres what the Church is called to do all

the time, which is to make known the good news in such a way
that men will respond.

The parish priest will, then, plan his preaching over a year so
that the great acts of God for man's salvation are declared and
explained, as on the festivals of Christmas, Good Friday, Easter
and Whitsunday. He will preach at times on the various marks of
the Christian life; he will teach about prayer in its many forms.
From time to time he will ask the regular churchgoers to do
something which will encourage those who do not belong to
come and hear the central truths of the Christian faith explained.
On those occasions, the priest will try to preach in such a way
that his hearers will make an act of decision to turn from self to
Christ. Very occasionally he may invite some other preacher to
share in this work, for the benefit of the regular congregation for
whom his own preaching may have lost its freshness. A familiar
means of undertaking this is through a Guest Service. Regular
church-goers are asked to take personally an invitation to a
friend or neighbour to come to such a service with them; alternatively an Area Leader and his helpers may visit all the homes
in their area with such invitations. Opportunity should be
given to the members of the congregation to indicate an act of
response, perhaps by asking for some leaflet which points a further
step or by meeting with the priest or trained lay counsellor for
some further talk.

Helping an individual inquirer to trust in Christ as both
Saviour and Lord is the highest privilege and greatest responsibility of any Christian, and it is part of the work for which a
priest is set free and to which he is ordained. No two souls are
alike and there is no technique which can be universally applied,
but there are some truths about God and man which are unchanging. It is of the essence of the love of God that he loves us in
spite of our sins, and it is of the nature of man that no one is
without sin. Thus when the priest is talking to the inquirer, it is one
sinner talking to another. It is of the nature of God that there is no
limit to his love, and the Cross is the assurance of this. If sin is

going our own way and saying No to God, then the Cross is human sin focused once and for all. Conversion does not depend on any one particular interpretation of atonement but it does involve seeing sin in the light of the Cross. It is of the nature of the love of God that no one is excluded and that whoever comes to Christ will not be cast out. There is also a uniqueness about Christ in that there is no other by whom man can be saved.

The inquirer may not take more than one step at a time and it would be very unwise indeed for the priest to force the pace or to prolong the interview. He relies on the fact that Christ himself is seeking the inquirer and he will say this to him. Yet, though the priest does not try to take the inquirer further than he is ready to go, he will not let the first meeting be vague and indefinite. The priest will help the inquirer to sum up the questions raised and the insights given, and they will pray together. This prayer may be anything from a full commitment of the inquirer's life to Christ and an acceptance of Christ into his life if he is ready for this, to a prayer for light in darkness and guidance into the way of truth. Some reading matter to help in the next steps in the Christian life will be given, together with some definite and simple instruction about prayer. If there are still questions and problems, a further meeting may be arranged. In the course of the meeting the inquirer may have admitted things of a very personal nature. The priest must therefore at the outset assure him that nothing he may say will be repeated or revealed to anyone at any time. Equally, however, the inquirer may need to make restitution to some one or to try to make his peace with another. Normally it is right for the inquirer to do this himself, but family quarrels can exist where a third party alone will be believed and the priest can act as mediator and take the first step; the inquirer must ultimately make his own peace. When the inquirer has left, the priest will pray for him and for those most closely involved with any step that he may have taken.

The inquirer needs assurance that even with his sin he can come to God, and that his sin will be forgiven and taken away. The priest will naturally point to the scripture to give this assurance. He will declare that fact of God's forgiveness with all the authority he can call upon. If the inquirer has no previous links with any church, that authority will come partly from scripture and partly from the personal testimony of the priest (as from one sinner to another) that he knows this to be true himself. Ultimately it can only be accepted by faith. If the inquirer was previously linked with the Church but has fallen away and allowed the link to be broken, the priest may explain the ministry of sacramental confession. He will explain that it is God alone who forgives sins but that this particular means of grace gives outward assurance of that forgiveness; it deepens penitence and clarifies the act of confession, and enables him to know that he is renewing his link with the visible Church and making a new start in its fellowship. The priest will remind him that what is forgiven is taken away and that, except when some restitution is due or a personal relationship needs to be adjusted, the inquirer must himself leave his sins behind. There is, in fact, a sense in which he must forgive himself as well as accept the forgiveness of God, not treating himself severely when God is merciful.

The formal use of sacramental confession will not only be exercised on such occasions. The priest must be ready to help any penitent soul who seeks assurance of God's forgiveness in this way and wishes to renew his relationship with the Church before coming to the Holy Communion. The words of his ordination give him this responsibility and authority in the Church. Some communicants are accustomed to make a regular confession in the presence of a priest at monthly or even shorter intervals. For them it is a part of their spiritual self-offering, and if they move to a new parish (which is becoming more and more part of the pattern of life) they hope to find this ministry available. Behind their practice there is an awareness that there are things which the Church declares to be wrong and, in having done these wrong things they have weakened the witness of the Church. There are others who, in addition to this approach, turn to their parish

priest as a Director of Souls for regular guidance in the development of their prayers. Others may very seldom take advantage of
this ministry but value it greatly at an annual retreat or at the
major turning-points of life.

From time to time the priest should read to the congregation
the first Exhortation in the Holy Communion service and explain
what provision he makes for those who wish to take advantage of
its offer. The people should know where and when they can come
to unburden their conscience and receive absolution and counsel.
Convenient occasions to read the Exhortation and to remind the
people of this ministry are before the major festivals of the
Christian Year. Even in parishes where the very mention of the
word 'confession' conjures up feelings of a violent sort, an
assurance that the priest will be in church at certain times for
anyone to see him to unburden their conscience, or to seek
advice, is accepted as part of his duty. Some people come and
tell of their sins and need to be told by another person, who is
commissioned to do this, that God does forgive them.

The priest will explain, perhaps in a sermon, how this ministry
of reconciliation is exercised. He will point out that he may not at
any time reveal to any other person, however closely connected
with himself or the penitent, anything of what is told him when
he hears a confession. If he talks about this ministry during the
preparation of confirmation candidates, he will explain that this
means he will not warn their parents about anything that they
may at any time confess. (Elderly and sick persons may need to be
told that this seal of confidence applies after their death.) If the
priest does talk to young people about this ministry then he is
wise, in my opinion, to tell their parents that he is doing so; this
can be done quite naturally when the parents meet together
before a confirmation. The priest, in describing this ministry,
will explain in complete detail exactly what happens when such
a confession is made.

Normally the priest will hear a confession, except of a patient
who is in bed or housebound, in church and it is easiest if a

faldstool is provided with a printed form for use by those who come. The place in the church where confessions are heard should be easily found and yet not so obtrusive as to arouse the curiosity of an inquisitive visitor; if there is a side-chapel, this is an ideal place so long as those who may come know where to go. It is convenient if the priest, wearing cassock and surplice and purple stole, sits facing away from or at right angles to the penitent, not looking directly at him. It is to God Almighty that confession is made, and the circumstances in which it is done and that on which the eye may rest should not detract from this. The priest will give a blessing in his own words or use some prayer such as 'The Lord be in thy heart and on thy lips, that thou mayest rightly and truly confess thy sins'. The priest then listens, reserving all questions if possible until the penitent has finished, and then asking a question only if it is necessary to clarify what has been said. Counsel to help the development of character and the receiving of grace to resist the temptation to which the penitent is prone can be given, and an act of penance given. The penance is not a payment or penalty for the sins confessed; Jesus Christ has himself carried the cost of all our sins. The penance is an act of love and thanksgiving to God and should be such that it can be carried out almost at once. The priest remains sitting for the absolution, which he gives in the form in the service for the Visitation of the Sick in the Book of Common Prayer. 'Our Lord Jesus Christ, who hath left power to his Church to absolve all sinners who truly repent and believe in him, of his great mercy forgive thee thine offences: And by his authority committed to me, I absolve thee from all thy sins, In the Name of the Father, and of the Son, and of the Holy Ghost. Amen.' The 1549 Prayer Book added 'the same form of absolution shall be used in all private confessions'. The priest then gives a blessing.

The counsel given should be short, and it may be necessary to ask the penitent if he would, at some time, like to talk over his rule of prayer or any other matter he may wish. It must be quite clear, however, that absolution closes the matter of the sins confessed; any further counsel relates to the future of a forgiven sinner. Clearly the nature of the counsel given will depend, to some extent, on whether the penitent comes regularly to the priest or regularly goes to some other priest. The priest is likely to have people coming to him who want counsel, but have no immediate intention of making any formal confession. They should make this clear when they come to him if for no further reason than that of timing the interview, lest some other person be wanting to make a confession.

The word 'counsel' has acquired overtones of new meaning in recent years. It must be non-directive and non-judgemental. If this rules out 'looking unto Jesus' on the part of the priest or pointing the inquirer to the grace of God, then the priest will find it hard to be 'non-directive'. If, however, it means acknowledging the maturity of the inquirer and his responsibility to make his own decisions without becoming dependent on the priest, then the priest's counsel can be non-directive. If to believe that all sin is an offence against a God of love, and to believe (and say) that the most bestial sinner is the object of the infinite love of Christ who died for us 'while we were yet sinners', is to be judgemental, then the priest is judgemental. If it means that the inquirer is not rejected because of his actions or his problem, this has been part of the good news of the Church for nearly two thousand years, though it has not always been practised as it should. There are many groups of people, Probation Officers, Marriage Guidance Counsellors and others, whose training sets a high professional standard of counselling. They may be non-judgemental of persons, but they have standards and aims. The belief that 'the well-being of society is dependent on the stability of marriage' is the foundation of the National Marriage Guidance Council. The priest must respect these counsellors and their standards, and be ready to commend inquirers to others who have special insights into their particular problems. Sanctified common sense is not sufficient to guide and strengthen a drug-addict or a homosexual.

If the priest sees that the inquirer needs specialist advice, he should encourage him to go to one who can give it.

Counselling is two-way communication. The counsellor's aim is to help the inquirer see his problem in a true perspective, arrive at his own interpretation of it and so see for himself a solution. The circumstances of meeting should be such as to put the inquirer at his ease. Even such small matters as allowing him to choose in which chair to sit can be important. The whole process must be 'client-centred', and the inquirer must never be allowed to place responsibility for success or failure on the counsellor. Equally, the inquirer must not transfer the blame for his failures on to God by being told to pray in some special way. Behind the scenes the priest will undoubtedly pray hard for the inquirer, but he will not use prayer at the interview either to preach indirectly ('help us to see that . . .') or as a kind of magic charm. On the other hand a priest has, and is known to have, convictions and standards, and it is because of them rather than in spite of them that the inquirer comes to him.

In practice, when the parish priest has come to be trusted by the people of the parish, he will be consulted by them on all sorts of matters on every level of difficulty. Mr and Mrs Jones want advice as to whether to send Mary to a church school or a more local county school. Mr and Mrs Smith have a problem: their daughter aged 15 wants to go on a camping holiday with her boy friend and another young pair. The Robinson children have got friendly with some Jehovah's Witnesses and the parents don't like it. Mr Thomas has left home again and Mrs Thomas has no money: what shall she say to her children? Mrs James has been widowed, and her family have moved away; she wants to talk out with somebody whether to stay where her roots are, or to move and start a new life somewhere else in more country surroundings. And so more and more people pose more and more problems. Sometimes they know perfectly well what the right answer is, but they want some moral support in choosing another way. The problems vary in size. The priest does not

wait in his study with fixed consulting hours and get visited only
by depressed people who need skilled psychiatric treatment. He
visits his people and is told of their hopes and fears, their joys and
sorrows, in ordinary conversation. Further, he has gone to them
and learns these things in their homes; they are talking on their
own ground. There will be five main themes which will arise in
the problems that are discussed. Sin relates to the past and is the
matter for confession in some form and for forgiveness by God.
Fear, doubt, weakness of will and breakdown of personal relationships account for most of the conversations relating to the future.
It is good that priests should be trained to recognise fears when
they are present, and that they should know enough about
personal relationships to point the way to healing. It is good that
they should be trained to think theologically about family quarrels.
It is good that the priest should see biblical parallels to the parochial
problems he meets. It is good also that by constant visiting and
listening to very small problems he may be able to allow parishioners so to talk about them that they are faced before they have
a chance to become large problems.

The remedy for fear and doubt and weakness of will is ultimately
to be found in the grace of God. The perfect love which casts out
fear derives from the love of God for us, which he has already
shown in Jesus Christ. Trust in a God who not only loves, but
has power to act now, is the true antidote to fear. The priest does
not use the occasion when an inquirer pours out his troubles to
persuade him to come to church, so that his congregation may be
larger. Equally he should not, in my opinion, be silent when he is
the ordained representative of that Body of Christ to which has
been given the secrets of man's salvation. If there are means of
grace by which the wills of men may be strengthened, then an
inquirer whose fears are due to weakness of will should be told of
them. This is not to reduce prayer or sacrament or faith to the
level of magic; it is to recognise the power of God's activity in the
world of today and to know something of the pattern of that
activity in the lives of men. It is likely that an inquirer who comes

to a priest for counsel has at least some belief in God. Even to one whose belief is uncertain, it is fair to ask whether he feels that only human resources are available in facing his problem.

There is a further truth which is revealed in Christ which the priest, or any other person who is called upon for counsel, knows and may feel it right to point out. The rightness of a course of action is not measured by its immediate and apparent success; the Cross is evidence that you do not make men love you by loving them in all cases. While the priest as a counsellor will not pass judgement on the inquirer as a person, and will work outwards from the inquirer and his problem, yet he cannot as a priest encourage the acceptance of a course of action which evades the real issue for the sake of a short-term solution. In all his work as a counsellor of souls, the priest needs to hold together two basic principles. On the one hand, he is a servant of Christ who uses him as an agent of his word and love and grace; on the other hand, the inquirer comes as a free person and must be free to make his own decisions which include the freedom to reject the grace of God. This applies in interviews in respect of a turning to Christ, to occasions of private confession and of personal counsel. Most of what the priest is told on such occasions is locked away from others and dismissed from his own memory also. Some is carried as part of his burden of intercession. Some remains hidden from the ears of men but is a continual inspiration and encouragement to the priest as he sees Christ's love revealed in the lives of men.

13

MINISTRY TO EXTRA-PAROCHIAL GROUPS

THE work of a priest that has been described so far has been that in the setting of an English parish. This has been deliberate because the majority of priests in England are engaged in the parochial ministry, and inevitable because the writer's experience has been predominantly in that field. There are, however, groups of people who cannot conveniently be served by the parochial clergy. These groups differ widely from people who are detached physically from the rest of the community, as in a ship afloat, to people who have a common interest, occupation or problem. Thus in some cases the people are very much the same as the rest of the community, but their context is different; in other cases the people have a common characteristic, such as actors or apprentices or ordinands. There are others for whom both the common characteristic and the context act as a means of distinction from those who are served by the parochial clergy. Several factors relating to the office and work of a priest are illustrated by the way the Church exercises this non-parochial ministry. The degree of isolation of the group affects the priest's links with the Church as a whole, and the special characteristic of those he serves may affect his ability to understand their thinking and feeling, or to speak to them in terms they understand.

One such group is formed by the armed forces, who are likely to be isolated physically and who have also a common life and task which separates them from those who live a settled life in a parish. The extreme case is that of a ship at sea, and as far back as the year 1147 King Stephen ordered that 'on board each ship, there shall be a Priest', which appears to be the first valid reference to the Naval Chaplaincy service, though chaplains landed with the Norman army in 1066. Understandably at the time of the Crusades, priests would be expected to be available for those who took up arms and the role of chaplain in the Orders of Chivalry is a reminder of this. The Service Chaplain of today serves a distinct company of men and women, often with their families; his cure is not unlike a parish outside the diocesan parochial system. Many units are overseas and in the Royal Navy, of course, some are physically isolated. Chaplains of all denominations are appointed by a Chaplains' Department. Badges of 'relative rank' are required to be worn by chaplains to all land forces of countries which are signatories of the Geneva Convention. This does not apply to the Fleet, in which chaplains wear uniform but no insignia of rank. All chaplains belong to their Service, they share the risks of war and the conditions of life of those to whom they minister. Their status of equivalent rank can be overstressed. Either the chaplain shows the marks and qualities of a true priest, in which case his badge of rank is no hindrance; to the extent that he fails to show those marks and qualities, no amount of rank can compensate.

He quickly learns the way in which the men think, and the background against which they live. He shares the uncertainties which go with frequent postings at short notice, the broadening of vision which comes from travel overseas and the sensitive feelings which come from living and working in a land where one does not belong. In war-time, the chaplain is non-combatant but shares all the dangers of those he serves except those of aircrews over enemy territory. His task, as stated in Queen's Regulations, is to be available as friend and adviser to all ranks. This personal ministry, especially in war-time, is both wanted and respected; but the priestly ministry of gathering Christians into a visible form of the Church is equally needed and respected. Much of this, in a peace-time establishment, is very similar to what he might be doing in an English parish, with regular Sunday services including the Holy Communion and perhaps a rather formal Morning

Service, a Sunday School or Children's Church and some informal service followed by refreshments and discussion in the evening. In war-time, the strange conditions in which the Holy Communion was sometimes celebrated, in a Nissen hut or under the wing of an aircraft or just in the open air with the very simplest of outward forms, brought the men who attended and the priest himself to find a new depth and meaning in the broken bread and a new awareness of the presence of Christ. Further than this, the distinctions of rank and function which are a necessary part of service life are seen as things of earth at a communion rail; perhaps the very necessity and clarity of these divisions makes their breaking down in Christ all the more significant.

The chaplain has several distinct advantages over the parish priest, in addition to that of common membership of the particular Service. He personifies the presence of the Church in the unit in which he serves more obviously, as he is appointed for this very purpose. The risks of war, the separation from home which often happens, and the sense of community which is part and parcel of service life make communication between the chaplain and the men easier than it is in a civil parish. His presence acts as a judgement (not a condemnation) of the whole purpose for which the Services exist, and while a pacifist could scarcely act as a chaplain, yet what the chaplain stands for is the Kingdom of God in which violence has no place. Perhaps the rough rhymes of Studdert Kennedy reveal that the reconciliation of what is with what God wills is only to be found in the Cross of Christ. Certainly the insecurity of life and familiarity with death, the wickedness of war and the attempt to restrain evil by force, prompt men to ask direct and simple questions about the value of life and the power and willingness of God to intervene in the affairs of this world.

The chaplain serves on equal terms with priests and ministers of other Christian traditions, and while each is loyal to his own Church the conditions for working together in natural charity are as good as could be found. The scandal and stupidity of the divisions in the Church stand out clearly, especially in war-time. Separate services of thanksgiving after deliverance from a common danger do not make sense. Niceties of form, of rite and ceremony, are seen in a different perspective when a conscience is burdened and the time for repentance on earth is limited. Chaplains of all denominations are expected to stand for the same thing, to have a common language. They are equally expected to be men of God and irrespective of denomination are respected, not because they are good fellows but because they are godly men.

Very many units stationed in England are small and these are served by the local parish priest, who acts as an Officiating Chaplain. In peace-time, the fact that the officiating chaplain does not share service conditions is not too great a disadvantage, and many have been war-time chaplains. In a small way, the fact that the officiating chaplain is a civilian helps to make clear that the Church in the forces is not something different from the rest of the Church. This point is equally, if not more strongly, made clear when a bishop visits a unit served by a commissioned chaplain for a confirmation. Service chaplains form a branch within their own service, under the control of the Chaplain of the Fleet, the Chaplain-General to the Forces in the Army, and the Chaplain-in-Chief in the Royal Air Force. The Bishop of Croydon acts as the Archbishops' Representative with the armed forces. Within the Service there is opportunity for fellowship with other priests, for in-service learning and growth in prayer at the Chaplains' School, and many chaplains are able to establish links with the civilian church in the area where their unit is stationed.

Another context outside the parochial system, in which many priests are engaged, is the whole field of education. The varieties of ways in which priests serve is so great that justice cannot be done to this subject in a few paragraphs, and the involvement of the Church in education is long, intimate and complex. There are priests who are Professors of Divinity, there are priests who teach physics and mathematics. There are school chaplains, there are specialists in religious education and there are headmasters in holy orders. There are schools with several priests on the teaching staff, where there is also a chaplain. Clearly the ways in which these men exercise, and are considered to exercise, their priesthood vary widely. School chaplains differ sharply in how they view the gathering of a 'church' within the school community and how they minister to the whole life of the school and not merely to the individuals of which it is comprised. Their relations with the parochial clergy are not always easy, especially when they prepare and present for confirmation boys whose families have little contact with the Church at home. Their involvement with the life of the school makes contact with the local clergy in deanery and diocese often tenuous, but on the other hand in most cases their work could not be effectively done by the local clergy.

The degree of sharing the life of those to whom they minister is different from that of the armed forces, for the categories of masters and boys are more distinct than those of officers and other ranks. The distinction between their pastoral concern and that of non-ordained staff is far less clear. A good Christian housemaster certainly exercises a pastoral ministry, and in a girls' school this pastoral function is equally obvious. The mode of appointment makes it less obvious that the school chaplain, or the ordained schoolmaster, is sent by God to exercise his ministry in that context, yet the priest concerned is likely to be very aware of this sense of vocation. It is important that every priest should be able to turn to a bishop when the need arises. This he can do to the bishop of the diocese in which the educational establishment is situated and, in addition, the Bishop of Taunton exercises a general pastoral care for school chaplains.

Prison chaplains have clearly a different context and the two-fold character of the community they serve is more obvious than in any other. Thus, though the chaplain seeks to make real the Church in the prison and to show that it consists of all Christians in the place, the sharp distinction between staff and inmates presents him with particular difficulties. On the other hand, although the chaplain is appointed and paid by the Home Office, his character as a man who is sent into the situation is obvious; he does not just happen to be there. His personal ministry to individuals is self-evidently priestly. He is not called to identification but to presence. As Bishop Lloyd Rees, when Chaplain-General of Prisons, wrote, 'On the Cross, Jesus was there to be the means whereby those between whom He hung could be the persons they might have been'. The chaplain sees every man on reception and is able to visit men in their cells and in hospital, to share their recreation, to meet their families and he is given every facility to offer friendship. It is on the basis of friendship in an apparently unfriendly setting that the chaplain can establish his work as a priest. It is when he knows the men and the conditions in which they are obliged to be that he can pray for them and love them. It is when the prisoners can know the chaplain as a friend that they can trust him with their confidence and begin to believe that there is a God of love.

It is neither possible nor right to attempt to measure the value of any ministry by visible results. The temptation to do this, as in areas such as industrial chaplaincy work or marriage guidance, is strong and the fact that there are visible results makes the temptation stronger. That there should be results is to be expected and the writer has grounds to thank God for the evident working of the Holy Spirit in the lives of many whom he has confirmed while they were in prison or at Borstal. It is good that governors and other members of staff on duty should make their Communion with the men. It is good that the work of the chaplain should be actively continued by the Church when the men try to re-establish their place in society, so that his work and that of the accredited voluntary associates in the Probation After-Care Service, that of the Prison Gate Mission in Liverpool (a unique enterprise where since 1879 men have received a welcome on their release), the Langley House Trust and the Guild of St Leonard, may be seen as part of the total caring ministry of the Church. As with chaplains to other specialised groups, it is important that the priest should have fellowship with other priests and that there should be a bishop to whom he can turn and who is known to pray for him and his work with understanding.

Hospital chaplains also serve in a community with a distinct two-fold character. An earlier chapter has already dealt with the priest's ministry to the sick which is part of every priest's ministry. The hospital chaplain is a specialist in that most of his time and care and prayer is concentrated on this one aspect of a priest's work. His presence as an integral part of the hospital staff points to a dimension in the work of making whole which must never be overlooked. His work has a further characteristic for, while there is this two-fold nature in a school or a prison, in a hospital one half of the community is changing fairly rapidly. In hospitals which cater for patients who may be there for months or years the chaplain's work will be adapted accordingly. In such hospitals the ability to realise the Church in that place, to make visible a eucharistic community and to have some sense of fellowship, is increased. It is not so easy to have much expression of corporate fellowship in Christ when Holy Communion is ministered to one patient in this ward and two in that ward. The chaplain is likely to feel a great sense of responsibility, and it can also be a sense of joy, in ministering what may prove to be the patient's last communion on earth.

The hospital chaplain does not minister only to the patients. The whole hospital is an outward and visible expression of the value which is placed on human life, and the Christian faith is directly concerned with the work of the individual. Thus he ministers to the medical and nursing staff and will co-operate with them by his manner, his quiet encouragement, his courtesy and his prayers. It is true that he is there by right, as part of the hospital staff, but his access to the patient can only be natural and quietly easy if he gains the confidence of the ward sisters and nursing staff. He ministers also to relations, especially at or near the time of death; but his ministry at this point may have to be passed on to the local parish priest where the patient's family lives. It is in this area of communication that the relation between the hospital chaplain and the parochial ministry needs delicate adjustment. The hospital is not a community apart and the fact that local clergy are encouraged to visit patients from their parishes is evidence of this. Equally the hospital chaplain must not be a person apart but seen as a colleague and friend of the local clergy. If this is so, he can exercise a ministry to the Church in the area; from his experience as a result of concentrating his attention on one aspect of priestly work, he can help his fellow clergy to exercise that part of their ministry better. Small hospitals are normally served by a part-time chaplain among the local clergy; indeed, to qualify for a whole-time chaplain a hospital must be of a size where, in fact, two priests would have more than enough to do.

14

MINISTRY TO SPECIAL
INTERESTS

THE basis of the work of the Service Chaplain, the school, prison or hospital chaplain, is that where people are there the Church should be. These communities are largely self-contained and it is not practical, and in many cases not even possible, for the parochial clergy to provide the pastoral care that is needed. Other communities and groups of people are far less self-contained. There can be community of interest, occupation, need or a common characteristic, which calls for particular pastoral care which can be given from outside. The single-handed parish priest will be able only to scratch the surface of this problem, but in a parish with a staff or in a team ministry special care will be given to special people. This is done in any parish where one member of the staff exercises pastoral responsibility for young people, or the over-60 club, and so on. The Police or the Fire Service, or the Passenger Transport Corporation of a city, provide a community of concern and interest. The individual officials of these services are all parishioners somewhere, and thus their pastoral care is the concern of some parish priest; but their life is bound up with their work more than most parishioners. In a city parish one of the parish clergy can exercise particular concern, say, for the Transport Department. He will come to know the bus crews, just as the parish priest comes to know his people. He will ask about, and pray for, their families. He will know those who organise the department. He is a priest and not a welfare-worker, though his knowledge of the family anxieties of a driver or conductor may help when problems arise. Naturally as he goes about his work he will come to know about routes and working conditions, but it is as an acknowledged representative of the Church exercising its ministry of caring that such a priest does this part of his work.

Shops and offices take men and women from their homes for the greater part of each day and a city parish which can maintain a pastoral ministry to the city stores supplements the work of the more surburban parishes. Theatres and night-clubs, however, are more nearly small communities of their own and the mobility of actors and dancers adds to the special nature of their need. Thus is 1899 the Actors' Church Union was formed to provide pastoral care for those engaged in theatrical and allied entertainment. The chaplains are welcomed and accepted just because they are priests. Their concern is a pastoral care for the souls of those to whom they go rather than a prophetic one about the rightness or otherwise of certain forms of entertainment. It is not necessary to condemn or to approve of strip-tease in order to express the concern of God for the girls who are employed in the night-clubs of our cities. The chaplains, wearing the outward uniform of a priest and carrying in their hearts the love of Christ, are able to go in and out of the night-clubs to exercise their ministry. They minister to theatres and cinemas and circuses, in which the hours of work dislocate traditional home-life. No parish priest on his own could minister to the needs of a family attached to a travelling fair or circus, living in a caravan in a different town every week. The fact that the chaplains are acknowledged and authorised by the Church as a whole enables them to be accepted; the fact that they are priests enables confidences to be given that otherwise would not be given.

It would be impossible to cover all the fields of human concern and activity in which priests are engaged, and in which they feel called to exercise their priesthood. There is a ministry to holiday camps, there are priests engaged in beach missions and other forms of evangelism. There are priests who work for charit-able and missionary societies, not because they are better money-raisers but because it is part of the Christian's duty to have a care for these things and to grow in generosity, and they help churchmen to grow in this grace. There are priests attached to television centres, there are youth chaplains, and general secretaries of synod committees and councils. The list would be almost endless. But there are two allied fields in which priests are engaged which bring out sharply two facets of priesthood.

Industrial chaplains and priest-workers both minister to those engaged in industry. The industrial chaplain may see himself as a pastor, but many of them value their ministry because it gives them an opportunity to serve the structures of industry and not merely those who are employed at any one moment. In the work of the industrial chaplain there is both a pastoral and a prophetic aspect. Before such a chaplain can begin his work, the goodwill of both unions and management is necessary; where this goodwill is available, the chaplain can go into an industrial concern without being identified as belonging to either side. To exercise any pastoral ministry at a personal level to even a small number of people in a large industrial complex may take months of patient visiting. The chaplain is able to call groups into being which cross the union–management frontier, to run weekend courses and other projects and in these to exercise a ministry in which mutual understanding is established. This he can reasonably see as a ministry of reconciliation. To effect such a ministry, however, there must be and be seen to be real independence. The industrial chaplain and the worker-priest do not exercise an identical ministry and comparisons are not relevant. The plea, so often made by those who encouraged the French worker-priest movement, that it is the Christian presence that matters, applies to both worker-priest and to industrial chaplain. Both are present but in different roles. Christian presence, however, is not a passive presence; in an imperfect world, that which reveals God brings both judgement and grace. Thus the industrial chaplain, who is allowed to be present in the British industrial scene, is bound to have some prophetic role. Either by what he himself says, or by the thought he provokes in others, he is able to bring to bear Christian insights upon the processes of decision-making and to open men's eyes to a dimension which might be overlooked. The ordinary parish priest does not normally have the time or opportunity to acquire the involvement of the industrial chaplain, and the worker priest does not have the detachment to exercise this prophetic ministry or this ministry of reconciliation in the same way.

Industrial chaplains are accepted because they are ordained. It is true that there are exceptions, as in the case of Franciscan Brothers or Church Army Captains, but it is the authority and commission of the Church which enables the chaplains to enter the premises at all and to be accepted by both sides of industry. It is rightly said that this reflects the fact that there is less anti-clericalism in this country than in many others. This welcome extends to all denominations, and Industrial Mission Teams commonly include ministers of several Christian traditions. The situation which obtains among chaplains in the Armed Forces obtains here; what the churches tend to regard as a happy venture in co-operation is seen by the world as evidence that in working together they are doing what they should be doing all the time. The fact that they are not overtly seeking to build up semi-churches within the factories, or to establish eucharistic cells, avoids at least one of the stumbling-blocks to co-operation. Thus the co-operation of ministers in this work, and in such spheres as television, exercises a ministry to the Church; it enables the Church to express its life and work ecumenically and so more easily become what it should be, which is the working of the grace of God.

In contrast with the industrial chaplain, worker-priests deliberately accept the role of manual workers. Those who are so engaged see this as their life's vocation with no intention of accepting promotion above that of charge-hand. Thus they share the tensions and clashes of loyalty, the frustrations and the fears of unemployment, that are part of the life of the weekly wage-earner. The number of such priests in England at present is small, and most are members of a group of worker-churchmen;

this group includes both priests and laymen. They recognise the great division between the organised Church, with its middle-class emphasis, and the vast majority of manual workers. In their desire that the Church should be present among these workers, they see the Church as including both priest and laymen and so their aim is the presence of priest and Christian layman among the manual workers. The priests who accept manual employment do so not to save and rescue individuals nor to create some half-way Church; as in the French worker-priest movement, it is the Christian presence that matters and that presence must be provocative by its holiness. The identification must be as far as possible real and permanent. There is here some parallel with the Religious Life. If at any time, as in a period of short-time working, the worker-priest is seen to be able to avoid the risks of unemployment by escape into paid parochial work, the identification would be incomplete. In fact many of the worker-priests do exercise an auxiliary pastoral ministry by helping in a local parish on a voluntary basis at weekends and in the evenings. It is, however, in the context of their daily work that they see their ministry, their priesthood, fulfilled. They are able from within the structure to view questions about the nature of man and freedom and moral choice differently from those outside. Some see the matter of language and thought-form as of vital importance. The highly practical and less articulate worker thinks and speaks differently from the average churchgoer, let alone the average priest. To express the gospel to such men involves being able to speak their language and to be sensitive to their feelings. There is a reverse process. If manual workers do not listen to the Church because they do not think in its language and thoughtform, so the Church does not listen to the workers for the same reason. The industrial chaplain and the worker-priest, each in his own and different way, can interpret to the Church as a whole why union members think and act as they do. Perhaps this task could and should be done by laymen, and both worker-priests and industrial chaplains should look ahead to the time when neither are necessary.

As things are in this country, that day seems far away. Meanwhile this task of interpretation, which is a ministry of reconciliation, is part of the total priestly activity of the Church.

The difference between the approach and work of the worker-priest and the industrial chaplain illustrates an important question about priesthood as a whole. This is the question of identification and separation. There is in ordination a certain 'setting apart' for the life and work of a priest; it is more than authorisation to perform particular functions. On the other hand there is a need to be alongside those to whom one ministers, to sit where they sit and to speak the language they speak. Either can be taken to an extreme, and when this happens the image of priesthood is distorted and the effectiveness of the priest to minister is reduced. Thus an over-emphasis on setting apart can develop into a false show of assumed holiness. Genuine contact with those to whom God sends the priest is lost, and he ends up surrounded by a small coterie of like-minded lay people. Over-emphasis on identification can lead to playing down the distinctiveness of a man's vocation. A typical illustration of this was the chaplain in war-time who was so anxious to be seen as a man's man that his work as a priest suffered. There is no standard formula to resolve this tension and each priest must find the balance which is right for him, but the existence of the tension is part of the life of a priest. Identification is by no means always necessary or possible. What is essential is a sensitive understanding and love of others for Christ's sake. Some measure of sharing can help, as in the case of wearing uniform in the services; on the other hand, the RAF chaplain does not need to be able to fly in order to establish a good relationship with the pilots. Differences of activity are expected, and the chaplain whose life speaks of God and who is known to pray for those he meets needs no further identification with those whom he serves. But the opportunity to meet and to speak a common language is essential if the priest is to exercise a valid pastoral ministry. Challenge and encouragement, judgement and grace, must go together. The priest who has too few points of contact with those whom he serves gives them little encouragement; his life has little meaning to them, being irrelevant to their situation. The priest whose life shows no evidence of that holiness which the grace of God works in the souls of men has no judgement to offer except by word of mouth.

This tension between involvement and detachment in the life of a priest is but one special example of the same tension in the Church as a whole. In biblical language it is the balance between being in the world but not of the world. If the Church is too detached from the world, concerned with details of its own life and unconcerned about the needs of the world, it will be judged irrelevant; if, on the other hand, there is no distinction in the quality of its fellowship and the service it offers to the world's needs, it will be regarded as one society among many others which men may join if they happen to like its ways. Yet the activities of the Church should stand both as challenge and as encouragement to the world. In its worship, which to an unbelieving world may seem irrelevant, it is declaring the glory of God and pointing the way to man's right relationship with God. Praise, thanksgiving and penitence are what man should feel and express before God. In its worship, the Church is continually being renewed. The truths of the incarnation, death, resurrection and abiding presence of Christ are all focused in the central act of the Holy Communion. Thus on the one hand, through its worship, the life of the Church is hid with Christ in God. On the other hand, the Church has a concern of mission and service to the world; its concern is to serve the needs of the world at their deepest level. In some ages, it was through the agency of the Church that most men's needs, material and spiritual, were met. Today there are many agencies, not all avowedly Christian, which do this work; in an age when only a minority of men can be regarded as churchmen, this is right and inevitable. This does not excuse the Church from its role of service as a Church, even though many Christian people will exercise their ministry of service through secular organisations. Unless the Church is involved, and seen by the world to be involved, in the service of men's needs it will be condemned by the world. Yet one of the greatest needs of the world is to discover the secret of corporate living, and this secret—the fellowship of the Holy Spirit—has been given to the Church to declare and share. By the divine quality of its fellowship the Church stands in silent judgement on the world, for it reveals what the world lacks; it also stands as encouragement to the world, for the harmony which the world lacks can and does exist. It should be said that, by its own divisions, the Church denies the good news it is charged to declare and lacks the fellowship it is given to share.

As the priest is ordained to represent the Church to itself and to the world, this tension must necessarily show itself in his life. In his prayer and his leadership of the worship of the Church his life will be directed to God; there will be an 'otherness' about it, not essentially different from that of a laymen but of a type which can be recognised by others. Equally the priest will be involved in the affairs and in the service of the world, a service directed by the vision of the Kingdom of God. Acknowledging the sovereignty of him who calls, and relying on his enabling power, the priest lives and prays and works for the acceptance of that same sovereignty in the hearts of man and in the structures of society.

15

THE MAN OF PRAYER

THE training of a priest is directed to the end that he shall think and pray theologically. It would be tragic if priests were the only people expected to do this. Indeed, it is because all are called to do so that the priest is so trained that he, in his turn, may teach others. Christian people have a right to expect that they can turn to a priest for help and guidance in prayer, and the priest should be able to explain how different aspects of man's faith in God can be expressed in prayer. His own pattern of prayer will be based on what he believes about God. Adoration will express his delight and wonder at the beauty and glory of God. His meditation will depend on his faith that God reveals himself to those who wait on him with reverence and patience. His thanksgiving will express his awareness of the active goodness of God, and his penitence will express his awareness of and contrition for his own share in the sin of the world. His intercession, and the confidence with which he makes it, will reflect his belief in the way God acts within his own creation. As the priest grows in prayer, so he grows in his vision of God and is able from first-hand experience to point the way to others.

There are, however, some special difficulties which affect the priest's life of prayer and also certain special responsibilities which are his. One of the difficulties arises from the fact that he is a professional. He is asked to say grace at dinners of all kinds, to open the meeting of the Parochial Church Council with prayer, to close the choir practice, to take an epilogue for the youth club, and so it goes on. At public services, he is the one who says the prayers; the congregation has no idea what is coming and has to do its best to enter into what the priest says. This familiarity with formal prayer carries its own dangers, and the sensitive priest is painfully aware of them; he knows that there are certain collects which are appropriate to a wide variety of occasions, and he knows the dangers of working these simple and grand prayers to death by constant repetition. This danger of meaningless formality can be avoided only by a deep personal well-spring of prayer. This, in its turn, depends on personal discipline, since the varieties of the calls made on a parish priest's time make it more difficult to know in advance what times can be set aside for personal prayer.

The requirement that every priest shall say the Daily Office of Morning and Evening Prayer is an invaluable help in such personal discipline. Whether the priest is in the mood or not, whether alone or one of a staff, and whether or not he personally values the practice, the saying of the Daily Office is part of his duty. The rubrics in the Prayer Book instruct him to say the office in church, and cause the bell to be tolled. The practice has far more value than mere discipline, though even at that level it is not to be despised. The priest who has been one of a staff and previously a member of a theological college where daily offices, and other forms of prayer, were said at fixed times knows how valuable that discipline can be. If he were not present for any reason, he knows that his absence will have been noticed—by man as well as by God. When he is on his own, in a sole cure without a colleague, his absence will not be noticed by man and the strength of his discipline is tested. The temptation to postpone the saying of the office to a later and hopefully more convenient hour presses on him, and only a man of strong will can do without the discipline of a regular place and time for the daily office. There are, of course, better reasons than mere discipline for the regular recitation of the office. The priest is part of a corporate company and the offices are the prayers of the Church of which he is a commissioned servant. As a priest, the life and activity of the Church are focused in him. The prayer of the Church is given expression as he offers to God Morning and Evening Prayer. This is more than doing what many others are doing at much the same time, though that is of value. The Bible Reading Fellowship, the Scripture Union and other similar bodies, derive much of their strength from the fact that hundreds of thousands of members are reading the same passage each day. Parish prayer groups and members of missionary societies have a similar strength if they use some common cycle of prayer and intercession. The value of the priest's daily office is to be found only partly in this. It is as the local expression and embodiment of the people of God that he offers the daily office; he is the Church praying in that place. If he can encourage others of the Church to be with him, this is even better. The danger of vain repetition and of absence of attention is always with him, but these dangers can be exaggerated. It is perfectly possible to have said the Te Deum without having praised God, or to say the General Confession without having been sorry for a single sin. This is a danger shared by the congregation on Sundays. If, however, one does say the Te Deum without praising God it is questionable whether any less disciplined act would elicit one's praise instead. The daily offices provide occasion to 'set forth (God's) most worthy praise, to hear his most holy word and to ask those things that are requisite and necessary as well for the body as the soul'. It may be right to revise the precise form of the office, but its value as an expression of the prayer of the Church can scarcely be exaggerated. In fact, the danger of vain repetition is more than offset by the help it gives for praise, thanksgiving, penitence, listening and intercession in those many moments when these do not come naturally and easily.

The use of a regular cycle of intercession comes easily when the daily office is said regularly. This may be the Anglican cycle of prayer, or some diocesan prayer calendar or parochial intercession list. In every such prayer list, there will be some matters of prayer which arouse familiar thoughts and some which are mere names on a piece of paper. Naturally the prayer will have more meaning to us if we know something about the places and the persons named, but the value of the prayer does not wholly depend on its meaning to us. These intercession calendars can widen our horizons of concern and we ourselves can benefit by becoming more conscious of our membership in a body which extends beyond our vision both in time and space.

The daily office can provide the priest with material for his regular meditation. If the written words of scripture are one medium by which God makes his Word known to men, then the lessons provide opportunity for the priest to pause and consider what God is saying to his people now. The lessons of the Old Testament point to the activity of God in the affairs of men. We believe that God is unchanging and there are sufficiently uncomfortable similarities between the events of each generation and some of the events of the Old Testament to affirm that mankind has many abiding traits. Meditation on the first lesson of the daily office need be no academic exercise, but instead may deepen man's faith in the power and will of God to exercise his lordship over history. Again the lessons of the Old Testament point to Christ in that their meaning can only fully be discerned in the light of the coming of Christ; those of the New Testament point to him by revealing the effect of his coming. Thus meditation on the daily lessons is a constant looking to Jesus which is one vital element in the life of prayer, whether of priest or layman. Another simple and valuable practice of meditation (especially suitable on a Saturday evening) is to consider prayerfully what difference would be noticed in the life of the priest himself and the parish he serves if men allowed God to fulfil the request in the collect for the coming week; the act of faith which provides ground for praying the collect, and the response needed in order that it could be answered, are added material for the meditation. Each priest, however, will have his own way of choosing how he will allow God to speak to him in his time of meditation and the matter he will use as a starting point.

If there is a danger of vain repetition in saying the daily office, there is more spiritual danger to the priest that in celebrating the Holy Communion frequently he may do so unprepared. Many priests are only too aware of this danger. This danger does not only apply to priests, for in parishes where the 'Parish Eucharist' is the main, and possibly the only, service on a Sunday it is all too easy for parishioners to come without adequate preparation. There is, it is true, a sense in which each Communion makes the Christian more prepared to come to the next. There is equally a sense in which no Christian is ever fully prepared. There is for the priest the added factor that he must celebrate the Holy Communion at some agreed times, whatever his spiritual state; the layman is free to decide whether to receive or to refrain. This freedom of the lay person is more apparent than real. It is not possible to withdraw from the judgement on human sin declared on the Cross, or from a share in the sin that placed Christ there. God will not exclude any man from the love revealed in Christ or the benefits of his passion. The Church, as the Body of Christ, cannot withdraw from its responsibility to make the memorial of the death and resurrection of Christ and with thanksgiving acknowledge his abiding presence. There is a special responsibility for the priest, in whom this priestly function of the whole Church is focused, to lead the Church in this activity; offering the Eucharist and receiving the Communion are not finally divisible. At the priest's own ordination, when he was given the privilege of being the spokesman of the Church in offering the Eucharist, his first act was to receive Communion; at every Eucharist that he offers, he also receives, though it may be three times on a Sunday morning. He may bring to these his personal occasions of thanksgiving, penitence and intercession. There are the many mercies of God for which the Church has reason to be thankful, the sin of the world in which he has his continuing share, and the grace of God for which all men have a continuing need, and in celebrating Holy Communion again and again the priest can identify himself with the thanksgiving, penitence and prayer of the Church and receive grace from God to be more thankful, penitent and prayerful. This does not absolve the priest from the duty of self-examination or of personal preparation for celebrating and receiving the sacrament, but it does enable him to use each Communion as a means of grace by which he is more prepared to celebrate and receive again.

There are times when Communion is celebrated with a special intention of which all the participants are aware. At a wedding, or on the dedication festival of a church, on the day of a funeral or on some special day of prayer, priest and people come with a common intention. Many more are the times when this is not so. The priest can, without obtruding his own concerns and responsibilities on the people, have his own special intentions at any Eucharist. Thus there may be in a parish a couple who have just been married, a new teacher appointed to the school or a lad who has lost his job for dishonesty. All these are parishioners for whose pastoral care the priest is answerable to God. Each is a reminder to him of his failures and his sin: it may be his half-hearted preparation of them for confirmation, his perfunctory contacts with the school or his own sinful desires and actions so similar to those of which one of his parishioners has been found out. He is thankful for the joy of the newly wed and for the love and trust that is theirs, for the skill and patience of the teacher, for the loyalty of the unfortunate lad's parents. As he receives the pledges of the abiding life and presence of Christ, so he prays that their lives may be transformed by Christ. He prays that the presence of Christ, so real to him and to those who share in the Communion, may be known by those for whom he especially prays as he offers that particular Eucharist. No one else may ever know of this intention, but the mercy of God is such that he does use this action of the priest to extend his grace to those for whom the prayer was made.

In addition to any personal intention the priest may have when celebrating the Holy Communion, he has a special relationship in prayer with those who receive. Together they make the sacrifice of praise and thanksgiving at which he is the spokesman of the Church, but when it comes to the administration it is he who ministers and the congregation which receives. The priest may find an enrichment and deepening of this if he mentally adds the Christian name as he uses the words of administration 'The body of Christ keep you (David or Mary, etc.) in eternal life.' His desire that all the benefits of Christ's passion may be received by each communicant is part of his ministry of intercession and part of his total intention in celebrating the Communion.

Because of his pastoral relationship with the people of a parish, the priest has particular duties of intercession. The general duty of the Church to intercede with God on behalf of men is made a particular duty for the priest. This is as much his duty as visiting the sick and burying the dead. The priest has a ministry of intercession which is both a privilege and also a means of identification with the people who are in need of the grace of God, and with the Church as the Body of Christ who shares their joys and sorrows, their hopes and their afflictions. It is Christ's love which constrains the priest to pray for the people, but with so many for whom to pray where can he start and finish?

For many of his people, the priest's prayer must necessarily be that of general intention. For example, by the time he has been five years in a large parish and married two or three hundred couples or presented a similar number of individuals for confirmation, his intercession cannot be other than general if these are to be remembered at all. However, if they are to be remembered, each priest should have his own system. Married couples may be remembered on the day of the month on which they were married; that is to say, a couple married on 17 May can be remembered on the seventeenth day of each month for the next few years. Later, they can be remembered on 17 May itself to prevent the daily list from being too cumbersome. The sick, the sorrowful, the homes of the newly baptised and many others can be remembered on a monthly basis. In a large parish such prayer cannot be too particular, but the priest can reflect on the daily list (and share it aloud if he has a colleague) before making his intercession on their behalf.

As he uses this longer list, the priest will want to make more detailed prayer for two or three persons of whose circumstances he has more intimate knowledge. One of the couples he married may be in a state of strain, a former confirmation candidate may seem to have fallen away from any expression of faith, a sick person may seem to have a terminal illness. God knows their needs better than any priest, and is more anxious than any created being could be that those needs should be met without violating their freedom to reject his grace. The priest, however, is placed in a position of pastoral relationship with these people and is called to be one channel by which the love and grace of God may be extended to them. In his prayer, therefore, the priest can reach out to God with faith in his love and power; he can picture the person for whom he prays in his particular need, and he can ask God to supply that need. If he knows the circumstances well, he can picture the person who is facing temptation or opportunity being aware of the presence of Christ and open to the grace and strength which it is his will to give. He prays, believing that his prayers are answered. It may be that, after so praying, the priest will feel impelled to visit or take some other step by which God can use him in the answering of the prayer that he has made, for prayer is neither a substitute for nor an escape from other pastoral activity.

This method of intercession can be used also by the priest in what is sometimes called 'praying his diary'. At the beginning of the day he may look ahead to all the known and probable activities that lie ahead, and envisage some of the many situations and people he will meet. The day is then pictured with the risen Christ as companion, present in every situation and at every meeting. His presence would bring courage in a moment of cowardice, restraint in a moment of hasty temper, gentleness in a moment of impatience. The priest will find it easier to recollect the presence of Christ at any time of the day, in its bustle and activity, if in a few moments of quiet withdrawal at its dawn he has renewed his faith in the fact that Christ will be there always and what that presence might mean to him.

The priest shares with readers, organists and choristers the fact that at almost every service of the church he is in the chancel, robed and sharing in the leadership of the worship while his wife and family are in the pew. However much they may feel that the act of worship is a common action of the Church, there is a divide between chancel and nave; one's attitude to the celebration of the Holy Communion is different when one is on the sanctuary side of the communion rail. For his own sake the priest is wise, if he can manage it, to go to the Holy Communion from time to time as a member of the congregation. This may involve going to some other church and, in country areas, where mid-week communions would be thinly attended, it is possible for three or four parishes to have a mid-week service in each church in turn. If the priest's wife and family can be with him, he and they can strengthen their unity and find some compensation for the enforced physical separation in church on Sundays.

Just as the priest will remember others on anniversaries of great events in their lives, so on the anniversary of his own ordination he will want to spend a time of recollection to thank God for the privilege given to him in this office and to reconsider his whole life and work. He may wish to go away to an organised retreat, or to spend a few days in quiet reflection. This withdrawal is but a means to enrich him for further service. One activity that will engage him during this period will be a prayerful re-reading of the ordination service, leading to renewal of the vision which prompted his call and a deepening of his commitment to Christ through the ordained priesthood of his church. He will offer his sins and failures, his apathy and cowardice, his lethargy and self-love, to God, looking to him for forgiveness and a renewed assurance of his power and commission to service. He will offer his thanksgiving for every sign of God's working in the hearts of those he has called him to serve. He will spend this time not so much revising a strategy for his work as refreshing his own soul and deepening his resolve, so that he may be a more faithful and useful messenger, watchman and steward for Christ.

The personal life of prayer, whether of a priest or of any other, is essentially personal and cannot be systematised by another. It is true that by virtue of the priest's involvement in leading public worship there are difficulties peculiar to the nature of his office, and by virtue of his pastoral responsibilities he has a particular duty to exercise a ministry of intercession. He also has a duty to say the daily offices of the Church. His own private walk with God and godly conversation are his own. What is sure is that his life and work cannot be separated. This means that just as his work gives him material for prayer and determines to some extent the direction of his prayers, so also his personal life of prayer will show itself in his work. His adoration and praise will show itself in a joyful life of service as surely as a young man in love reveals the fact to his friends. The priest's penitence will show itself in a gentleness with other sinful children of God, and his intercession in his devotion to the pastoral care of the family of God. His path through life, as seeing him who is invisible, will have a humility and a steadfastness which will overflow into his work of loving and caring for those whom he is called to serve. Unknown to him some may themselves turn to God in prayer having seen their priest, as the woman is recorded as having said of Elisha, the holy man of God who passed by continually.

16

BY WHAT AUTHORITY?

A PRIEST believes that he is called by God to declare his word and to minister sacraments which are means of grace. What authority is there in what he is and does and says? He not only assures men that God forgives sin but he says 'by his authority committed unto me, I absolve thee from all thy sins'. In law a man and woman marry one another, but the priest says 'I pronounce that they be man and wife together'. He goes to the scene of death and gives assurance of resurrection; he admits into the visible Church a new member through baptism. He declares in human words the Word of God and he gives in Communion what men receive by faith as the body and blood of Christ. In these several instances, the ground of authority is not the same. In a world where many familiar forms of authority are questioned, if not rejected, what kind of authority does the priest have and from where does it derive?

The Church of England is very clear, in the services of ordination and in the thirty-nine articles of religion, as to the place it gives to Holy Scripture as a source of authority in religion. The question asked when a man is ordained priest is quite plain. 'Are you persuaded that the Holy Scriptures contain sufficiently all doctrine required of necessity for eternal salvation through faith in Jesus Christ? and are you determined, out of the said Scriptures to instruct the people committed to your charge, and to teach nothing, as required of necessity to eternal salvation, but what you shall be persuaded may be concluded and proved by the Scripture?' The strength of this appeal to scripture is evident. Many great evangelists have based their message on the ground 'The bible says. . .'. They do not preach just what they think or what they have found to be helpful; they preach a message of salvation according to the scriptures. They do this, not because they believe it will be more effective, but because they believe it to be true. So long as the authority of scripture is accepted by the hearers, it will also be more effective. This is no accident. Part of the ground for accepting the authority of scripture is that by means of its message lives have been transformed into the likeness of Christ. This might seem mere pragmatism until the further question is asked, 'by whom are such lives transformed?' Preacher and hearer alike would agree that this transformation comes not from them, but from Christ the Living Word of God of whom the scriptures tell.

A problem at once arises, which has many sides. It is evident that preachers refer to certain parts of scripture with great frequency and emphasis, and to other parts with much less. Anyone who has responsibility for choosing lessons, whether as a member of a liturgical commission or as a parish priest arranging some local service, finds that he is exercising criticism; he chooses this and rejects that. Why should one book be chosen and another rejected? Is not *The Pilgrim's Progress* as inspired as the Song of Solomon? It is easy to say that *The Pilgrim's Progress* had not been written when the canon of scripture came to be accepted, but the principle remains. Why are some books 'scripture' and others not? By what authority does the preacher say 'the bible says'?

The early Christian Church inherited the scriptures of the Old Testament. These were Jewish scriptures, with laws applying to the Jews, with history of the Jewish people and promises of a Messiah. The early Church, however, was not entirely Jewish, and the relevance of Jewish laws for Gentile converts was an early matter of debate. The Jewish scriptures looked ahead to the promised Messiah, whom Christians acknowledged as Saviour not only of Jews but of Gentiles. As Jesus was Lord of both Jew and Gentile, so the scriptures which pointed to him were accepted by the whole Church and not merely by Jewish Christians. The law was described by St Paul as a schoolmaster to bring men to Christ. The Christian Church, however, preceded the New

Testament writings. They were the product of its life first and the guide of its life after. The good news was passed on first by word of mouth, by preaching; the consequences of the good news in personal and corporate living were passed on by teaching. Both these, preaching and teaching, were dependent on transformed lives. Christian faith is more than the sum-total of assertions about Jesus, but rather an inward experience which so transformed personal and corporate life that some explanation was necessary. The Gospels declare the Christ by whom the lives of men were touched and changed, and the Epistles arose out of the corporate life of such people.

Thus scripture and tradition, that which is passed on, reflect the ongoing life of the company of believers. The process by which Christian writings came to be accepted as scripture, with an authority equal to the writings of the Old Testament, was a long and gradual one. The process went on in every part of the early Christian Church, but not in an identical manner; for some centres of the Church used Christian writings which were later not universally accepted, while others did not acknowledge some which were later accepted. By the end of the second century, each Church had acknowledged some body of writings as expressive of its faith and life. By the time Athanasius wrote his Festal Letter for Easter, AD 369, the books which are now universally accepted as scripture were acknowledged as having authority for the Church. The distinction made between the books of the Old Testament and those of the Apocrypha, that is between those which are to be accounted canonical and those which are 'read for example of life and instruction of manners', is made by Saint Athanasius and is accepted in the Thirty-Nine Articles in the Church of England.

This determination of the canon of scripture is not a matter of the Church, or its bishops, sitting in judgement on a collection of books and accepting some while it rejected others. The acknowledgement of certain writings as normative of its life went hand in hand with the development of that life. Nor is this a logical quibble, for the Spirit of Christ whose incarnate life is depicted and whose risen power is experienced is the source of the life and power and witness of the Church. Insofar as a Christian writing reflects the truth about Christ, it will be acknowledged by the Christian Church if that Church is guided by the spirit of Christ. The Church is the community in which the scriptures are understood and acknowledged to be true.

Church and scripture are not alternative authorities, as though either is infallible without the other or even an infallible guide to the other. Each is dependent upon the other, and both are dependent upon the living Christ. The priest or preacher who relies upon the authority of the scripture, 'The bible says. . .', cannot do this independently of the accumulated teaching and experience of the Church. The priest or preacher who relies upon the authority of the Church cannot do this independently of the teaching of scripture. The authority of the teaching and preaching of the priest is that it makes known Jesus Christ, of whom the scriptures speak and from whom the Church derives its life and power. But the interpretation of scripture calls for scholarship and the use of reason. The authority of the preacher who relies on the word of scripture would easily be challenged if it were shown that he was using passages out of context, or as support for assertions to which they had no relevance.

Human intellect and reasoning power is a gift of God, and a gospel of salvation for the whole man must be acceptable by his reason. This does not mean that a priest's authority rests upon his cleverness in regard to worldly wisdom. It does mean that the preacher has no authority when he says 'The bible says' if he is using the text to mean something other than its true meaning. But what is its true meaning? May not a passage, or a whole book, have a meaning and a message over and above that which its writer intended or understood? It is at this point that faith and reason come together, whether in harmony or conflict; for the scriptures are understood by reason and come alive through faith. Acts of faith may take men beyond the point to which reason can go, but the preacher may not go in the opposite direction.

There is an additional argument for an emphasis on reason in the present age, when human cleverness and scientific method are combining to extend man's mastery over nature. This mastery extends beyond the field of space-travel and technology. The influence of drugs on human motivation and will-power, the understanding of brain-washing and the breakdown of human personality, are challenges to any message of hope and wholeness which is not in accord with reason. The study of corporate human behaviour by scientific methods calls for moral and ethical demands to be supported by reason. Such demands may ask for self-sacrifice far beyond the limits of pure reason, but when demands have consequences which an understanding of human behaviour shows to be unreasonable, the authority for such demands can and will be challenged. Thus temporal circumstances, such as the growth of population beyond the point at which the earth's food resources are adequate, cannot be ignored when ethical judgements are made in some fields. Then unsupported reliance on the authority of scripture or Church or both carries little weight.

Quite apart from scripture or the authority of the Church or any accord with human reason, there is a sense of ultimacy for some people in certain circumstances. When men find themselves led or driven to a point of major decision, all that scripture and Church and reason and experience has contributed to their being is merged into one as they respond. The reply of Peter and John to the authorities recorded in Acts 4, verses 19 and 20, is an example of this; the declaration by Martin Luther is another. The dividing line between overwhelming conviction and bigoted obstinacy may not be easy to define, but there are occasions when overwhelming conviction occurs. Without attempting to analyse the psychology of conversion, there comes a stage when the Christ who is preached becomes for the Christian the Christ to whom total loyalty is given. There appears to be the action of the

Spirit of God upon the spirit of man, and for that man this action has its own authority. The doctrine of inner light, cherished so strongly by the Society of Friends, relies on a similar authority. In priest and layman alike this inner conviction affects, if not determines, the authority with which he speaks and acts to others. Excellence of speech and manner may deceive some hearers into thinking that a speaker knows what he says and means it; poverty of speech and manner may blind some hearers to the inner conviction of the speaker. It remains that sincerity, loyalty and personal conviction carry an authority which is recognisable and respected, even if the ground of that conviction is not accepted.

There is one further source of authority which belongs to the office of a priest as well as to laymen. The gospel which he is charged to proclaim and the mysteries of grace of which he is the steward relate to the risen and living Christ. The Church whose commission he holds is the Body of Christ. The life and words and work of a priest need to form a unity, from which it follows that his life must communicate Christ as his words and work do. The priest is called to represent the Church to itself, and to be a spokesman of the Church of the world. His life is seen by the world, and judgement of his life is judgement of the Church. Therefore as the Church is called to be holy, so the priest is called to holiness; so also is every churchman.

Holiness concerns a man's relationship with God, rather than moral uprightness, though clearly there are moral consequences. The priest who falls below certain accepted moral standards may expect a measure of publicity greater than that which would attend a non-churchman who had a similar lapse. This may be cruel, but it does reflect what the world expects of the officers of the Church. It may be that fear of publicity, and of others knowing, helps some priests (and lay Christians) to resist temptation which would otherwise be too strong for them. But holiness is a religious rather than an ethical quality. It denotes a sense of being set apart, yet without any of the unctious piety of the 'holier than thou' variety. Without ceasing in anyway to be entirely human, the priest is called to be a man of God. His life, his words and actions, should make it easier for others to be aware of the presence of God. Any sense of separatedness is not a denial of closeness to his fellow men, for the Holy God to whom he is called to be close chose to reveal his concern for men through the Incarnation. The priest's closeness to God will reveal itself in Christlikeness, and any Christlikeness he has will show itself in closeness to those to whom he is sent. Thus sympathy, or an ability to enter into the feelings of others, is a mark of Christian holiness. So also is an inner joy even in time of strain; it was for the joy that was set before him that Christ endured the cross.

This kind of holiness is easier to recognise than to describe. Its relation to wholeness is such that it belongs to the inner being of a man, and cannot be put on like a cloak. There is an essential integrity about it, and a depth beyond the vision of others. It is not so much an imitation of Christ as a life which is 'hid with Christ in God'. But this kind of holiness carries an authority; confronted with a real man of God, people are impelled to listen and take notice.

These five strands of authority, scripture and Church, reason, inner conviction and holiness, are interwoven. A Church in which any of the five is discounted is to that extent incomplete. This is to be expected, for each is evidence of the working of the one Holy Spirit through whom the grace of God and the life of Christ is mediated to men. None of these strands is restricted in any way to the priesthood. All Christian people are called to be holy and to have an inner conviction which reflects itself in total self-abandonment to Christ. The task of the priest is to lead the members of the Church, to represent to them what they are called to be. The authority by which he does this lies in no self-acquired qualities but in a combination of the five factors which are but a few of God's gifts to men.